#21

"I Never Stopped Smiling"

The Inspirational Autobiography of Kevin Daley,
Formerly known as Harlem Globetrotter Great
"Special K"

"I Never Stopped Smiling"

The Inspirational Autobiography of Kevin Daley, Formerly known as Harlem Globetrotter great "Special K"

BY: Kevin Daley

3DQUEST
California

First Printing, 2014

ISBN 978-0692237687

Cover designed by David Ellsworth

Cover photography by Jam-X

Back Cover headshot by Karine Simon

3DQUEST

Marina del Rey, CA 90292

Ordering Information:

Quantity sales. Special discounts are available on quantity
purchases by corporations, associations, and others. For
details, send an email to info@kevindaleyspeaks.com or call
(800) 708-3979.

www.KevinDaleySpeaks.com

To the one that always makes me smile no matter what.
Kaydee Veronica Daley, I love you with all my heart!

Table of Contents

I. I was Just Three Years Old 1

II. One Way In And One Way Out 19

III. I'm The First In The World 35

IV. Most Likely To Succeed 45

V. The Eyes Of My Murderer 57

VI. Wow, This School Is Big 62

VII. There Was No Romantic Music 70

VIII. There's A Surprise In There For You 88

IX. That Was Not My Life 94

X. You Just Keep Doing What You Doing 106

XI. I Just Couldn't Believe It 118

XII. What Are You Going To Do 133

XIII. I Dunked On Michael Jordan 150

XIV. Kevin "Special K" Daley Is Born 169

XV. Here Comes The Head 185

XVI. I Won 193

XVII. Represent From Panama 197

XVIII. He Never Stopped Smiling 210

XIX: 21 KEYS TO SUCCESS 220

"I Never Stopped Smiling"

*The Inspirational Autobiography of Kevin Daley,
Formerly known as Harlem Globetrotter Great
"Special K"*

Acknowledgments

I cannot express enough thanks to my family, friends and fans for their continued support and encouragement. I want to take this time to thank the many that there are, in no particular order. If you don't see your name here, please don't feel bad. It would take the entire book pages to be able to fit everyone's name!

Special thanks to my baby Kaydee, Toi, my father Alford Daley Sr, my brother Alford, my brother Sergio, my cousin Damian, all my other cousins, my aunts, my uncles, my nieces, my nephews, my Harlem Globetrotter teammates. I love you all.

Also thanks to all of my fans worldwide, Mr Michael Touhey, Missy, Mikell, Laura D, Coach Merino, Coach Hayford, Coach Tex Harrison, Coach Clyde Sinclair, The Harlem Globetrotters organization, Donti, Donte, Demetrious, Rhonesia, Diggs, Kathy and Keith Hollimon, Lenard, Manolo, Tia, my classmates from Instituto Episcopal San Cristobal, Yvonne Contreras, Carl, Marques Johnson, Bill Milliken, Will Moreland, Todd Ramasar, Nancy Lieberman, all of my friends in Panama, the United States and all over the world.

And last but not least, those who didn't believe in me. Yes, I thank you because you were a strong force of motivation for me.

Introduction

I've been through many things in my life - some positive, some negative. Somehow, the negative situations always stand out in my mind. For years, many of those negative issues were so hard for me to speak about. And it was certainly never my intention to share those negative things with anyone, let alone share anything negative that had ever happened to me in a book.

But then one day, I attended a program where teenagers shared their stories about horrific events in their lives. They talked about encounters they'd witnessed and experienced. The entire time I listened to them, I kept thinking, 'These are just kids!'

Hearing those young people changed my life. Watching them stand up and tell the truth of their lives motivated me. That was the day when I finally decided to share my story. I knew that I'd been through many things and had learned many lessons that could provide motivation to others. That was when writing this book became my dream, became my goal.

I was born in Panama, a very small country in the southern most part of Central America. I came to the United States at the age of twelve with nothing more than two small suitcases. Since that time, I've lived in five different countries and have travelled to more than ninety-five countries. It hasn't been entirely positive, but I know that every experience, every situation molded me into the man that I am today.

My hope is that as I share the experiences of my life, you will be inspired and motivated. I hope that inside the pages of this book, you will see through my life experiences, that you can overcome any adversity in your life. That is my true goal for writing *I Never Stopped Smiling*. I want to show that while challenges will come to all of us, there is nothing that you cannot face, there is nothing that you cannot overcome. Adversity is just a part of life - for everyone. That is why, while most of this book is about my life, I've added lessons that I've learned that I believe will help you overcome adversity and use every part of your life experience to succeed. I call these lessons the "21 Keys to Success." These are the key factors one should possess in order to succeed. How did I come up with twenty-one? 21 is the number I wore during my ten years with the Harlem Globetrotters; so it's only fitting, right?

My life is much more than this book, but I hope the stories and experiences that I share are entertaining, helpful and most importantly, motivating. I hope this book will give you guidelines to follow on your own journey to success.

I am not a writer by any means. I've been an athlete my entire life and I'm very proud of that fact. But one thing I can say after finishing this book -I am now an author!

I.

I was Just Three Years Old

"Tears are often the telescope by which men see far into heaven." -H.W. Beecher

I was born at 12:07pm on October 7, 1976, in Panama City, Panama, son of an accountant, Alford Benson Daley and a teacher, Melva Veronica Daley. My parents already had two children, two boys. So they were absolutely sure I was going to be a girl. See back then, it wasn't very easy to find out the sex of your baby before the birth, so my parents played the percentages. They assumed that after two boys, the next baby had to be a girl. 'Boy', were they wrong!

I'm not sure how big I was at birth or how much I weighed, but I assume that since today I'm 6'5" and 210 pounds, I must have been a larger than average baby.

Since my not being a girl caught my family by surprise, my parents didn't have a name picked out for me. Michelle, my cousin on my mother's side who was also born on October 7th but thirteen years earlier, thought it would be cool to name me after the male version of her name, Michael. Michael Daley? I'm not sure I would have liked that. But after contemplating that idea, Mom and Dad decided on Kevin Alexis Daley Hewitt.

Now, I know you're probably laughing at my middle name right now. Well, let me tell you - Alexis is a male name in Spanish speaking countries. Here in the U.S., it's considered a female name, although I have met a few American males with that name. But if you ask me, Alexis one of the manliest names you will ever come across!

Speaking of manly, my father was a proud man who began working when he was just a young school kid. He worked all kinds of jobs - from being a dishwasher at a clubhouse, to working as an accountant for the United States Air Force in Panama.

As serious as he was about work, my father was equally focused on his education. He was the oldest of his siblings, and because of hard work and focus he did well in school. So well, that it concerned his mother.

"One can't be wise and the others dumb," my grandmother told my father.

My grandmother was concerned that my father was getting too far ahead educationally from his sisters. That's crazy, huh?

So with my grandmother's encouraging, my father stopped school in the ninth grade and went to work. But he always intended to go back and, after two years, my dad did just that. Since he was working he chose to go to school at night. But he carried his work ethic into the classroom and he ended up graduating at the top of his class.

That was a proud accomplishment for my father, though he never felt connected to any school. To this day, he feels like he missed out on having an alma mater because it just wasn't the same going to school at night. He didn't have the same connections, nor the same activities - sports and social events - that he would have had if he'd never dropped out. But nonetheless, he completed his education and went to work at the Panama Canal Zone.

Not too long after graduating, he met my mother, Melva at a friend's baby's christening. My father was smitten with my mother, who was a junior at the University of Panama. She was majoring in Secondary Education and my father still talks about how she was so lady-like, so different than the women he knew.

"She wasn't an ordinary woman," my father says. He loved the way she talked, the way she walked; he loved her manner and the overall way that she carried herself. And she was easy-going, fun-loving.

She was also a beautiful woman, about 5'7" with a slender, model-like physique. Her smooth chocolate skin and bright brown eyes really attracted my father.

Now my father wasn't any kind of slouch either and he could definitely hold his own with his 6'2" frame. He wasn't a big guy, but you could tell that he was in good shape.

After that meeting, my parents dated for about a year before they married in 1969. They were very happy together and wanted to have a family right away. My oldest brother, Alford, Jr., was born in November of that same year. He was their only kid for three years, then, my other brother, Sergio was born in August of 1972. Four years later, I came along.

Of course, I remember little about the earliest years of my life, but when I was three, my life changed in a way that still impacts me today.

According to my father, it began about ten years after my parents had been married. My mother seemed to be down, depressed even and my father attributed her behavior to the fact that she was staying home all day. She was a high school English teacher and for the first time in her adult life, she wasn't working. The school system was on strike. So my father thought her unhappy state was a temporary thing.

But when my mother returned to work, she didn't go back to normal and my father knew that something was wrong. There were times when my mom just seemed 'spaced-out.' But then suddenly, she would come back. At night, my father would often stay awake and watch her, worrying and wondering about her the whole time.

After a few weeks of her being in this state, my father told her that he was concerned.

"What's wrong, Melva?" he asked her.

But my mother was never able to express what was going on inside.

Wanting to do all that he could for her, my dad took her to doctors, all kinds, including a neurologist and even a witch doctor. He was relieved when one doctor recommended a week's stay in the hospital. That made my dad hopeful; maybe during that time the doctors would find out what was wrong with her. Maybe they'd be able to get my mother back to normal.

Seven days later, my mother was discharged and so that she could have even more rest, she stayed with one of her brothers for another week.

But when she finally returned home, it seemed like the time she spent hospitalized hadn't helped. Just like before she left, there were times when she'd look at my dad as if she didn't know him. With nothing else left to do, my dad did the only thing he could. He turned to God. With lots of prayer, he left it all in the Lord's hands.

The beginning of the end came one night in November, four days before my oldest brother's tenth birthday. I was just three and don't remember the incident at all, but I was told that my father was awakened out of his sleep by my and my brothers' cries. When he rushed to our bedroom, he was horrified by what he saw.

My mother was beating my brother, Alford. She'd hit him so hard that there was a gash in his head that bled. Sergio and I were unharmed, at least physically. Sergio did have a small cut on his finger, but the major damage came from what we were witnessing.

My father grabbed my mother's arm, holding her back from striking Alford again.

"Melva!" he shouted. "What are you doing?"

She stepped back, away from Alford, but she didn't respond. She stood, staring at my father, her eyes completely blank.

It was our cries that my father focused on. He checked Sergio and I, to see if we'd been hurt. Then, he turned his attention to Alford, all the time, trying to get us to calm down.

His attention was on his sons. So of course, my father didn't see my mother rush from our bedroom. Of course, he had no idea that she ran into the kitchen, and slouched against one of the cabinets. And of course, he didn't know that she'd picked up a bottle of bleach and began to drink it.

It wasn't until my father quieted us down, that he realized my mother had left. And then just a moment later, we all heard a thud - the sound was my mother's body falling to the floor. She was completely out of it by the time my father ran into the kitchen. Foam oozed from her mouth and her eyes were rolled back. My brothers and I were terrified as my father ran across the street to our neighbors for help.

My brothers tell me that the rest of that night moved so quickly. The neighbors stayed with us as our father lifted our mom from the floor and carried her to his car. After he made sure that she was safe inside, he drove as fast as he could to the nearest hospital.

"Help me!" my father said when he rushed into the Emergency Room, carrying my mom in his arms.

It was a nurse who calmed my father down first and then got the doctors to help him.

"She drank bleach!" he told them.

I'm sure they had other questions that my father could not answer. Why would she do that? Why would she attack her own children?

The doctors pumped my mother's stomach and my dad sat in the hospital room with her. It was a few hours later when, with tubes injected into her arms and a single tube coming out of her mouth, my mother asked, "How's Alford?" Her voice was soft and groggy; my father told us that she was barely conscious. But she wanted to know if her son was all right.

It wasn't until the doctors told my father to go home and get some rest, that he left, rushing home to check on us.

Alford was fine; his injuries weren't serious. All three of us were fine - at least on the outside. It was just the shock and confusion that had a hold on us.

Our father got us back into bed and made sure we were asleep before he went to sleep himself. But he was up early, wanting to get to the hospital, wanting to make sure that my mom was okay.

But she wasn't.

My father found out as he was going up the steps leading into the hospital and my grandmother, his mother-in-law was coming out.

Her eyes were filled with tears when she shook her head and softly said, "She didn't make it. Melva didn't make it."

"No!" My father didn't want to believe it. He ran up the steps, and through the halls to the room where he'd left his wife. But there was no one in the room, no one in the bed. And he knew that what my grandmother had told him was true.

Our mother was gone.

The sight of the empty bed hit him and my father broke down in tears. The woman he'd loved was gone. She was gone forever.

***

I was just three years old when that happened, so I have no memory of that at all. Everything that I know about that night came from what my brothers and my father told me in later years. But not being able to remember that hasn't stopped my mother's suicide from affecting every single day of my life.

Not only do I not remember that night, but I don't have a single memory of my mother. All I know is what I've been told, and the only visuals I have are the pictures that she left behind, which seem to be so few.

So growing up, I felt abandoned; I was so angry with my mother for leaving me. I felt like she robbed me of having the love of a mother that every child deserves. Anytime I thought of her, it brought me to tears, but not tears of grief. I cried because I was angry. I was angry because it didn't have to be that way. She didn't have to do what she did; she chose to do it. And if she chose to do it, then that meant that she chose to leave me.

I had so many questions. I wanted to know why, if my mother loved me, would she leave me? Why had she been so selfish, why didn't she care about me? Why couldn't she fight through whatever she was feeling and be there for me?

It became particularly painful when I saw other kids with their mothers. That sight could sometimes break me to pieces. But I never shared those feelings with my friends. Not at all. I never even shared the truth with most of them.

As I was growing up, whenever anyone asked about my mother, I made up stories, telling kids that she lived in a different country. I just never could get myself to say that she was dead, and there was certainly no way that I was going to tell anyone that she'd killed herself.

Losing my mother, at such a young age, and in that way affected my friendships, my relationships, my life. My emotions were all messed up and really, I should have reached out to a psychologist. But I never did. At first, I was too young to know that I needed any help. And then, as I got older, I didn't think anyone could help me. So, I held on to all of those bad feelings and it wasn't until I was thirty years old that I finally made the decision to let it go. I had to. Holding on to all of that wasn't ever going to bring her back and I had to deal with that fact.

A good friend of mine recently told me that my mom probably did what she did because she loved us.

"But how can she do that if she loved us?" I asked, not understanding at all.

My friend explained, "Your mom loved all of you. She left you because she was terrified that she would hurt you. She sacrificed herself to keep you safe because there was an ugly part inside her that she couldn't control. She was desperate for help, but didn't know where to turn."

It took a moment, but those words made sense to me. I wish I had heard this many years ago. I don't know if what my friend told me is true, but at least the thought helps me deal with losing my mother a little better.

***

No one was untouched by my mother's death. My father was as profoundly affected as my brothers and I were. My dad's major concern after my mother's funeral was what was going to happen to his sons?

One day, soon after the day my mother left us forever, her mom asked my dad, "What are you going to do now?"

It must have been the way my grandmother looked at me and my brothers that made my father jump up. He grabbed Alford, Sergio and me and hugged us tightly. "I'm going to take care of my boys!" he said. "That's what I'm going to do!"

And that is exactly what he did. My father did his best to take care of us. But I was only three years old, and my father, in his desire to really take care of me, sent me to live with his mother in Colon. Colon is a seaport city about forty-nine miles away from where my father and brothers were in Panama City.

At first, I was excited to be away. My grandmother and my aunts (my father's sisters) showered me with all kinds of love. But it didn't take long for me to really miss my father and my brothers. It was bad enough that my mother was gone, but it now felt like my father was gone, too.

With my grandmother living so far away from Panama City, I didn't see my father and brothers too often, although my dad came whenever he could.

But one day, after I'd been with my grandmother for about a year, I cried and cried when my dad came to visit.

"I miss you," I told him. "I want to come home."

I don't know if it was the way I begged or if my father just thought it was time. Either way, I went home with him that night. And I can't tell you how happy I was to be back with him and Alford and Sergio.

It hadn't been easy for my father while I was away. In the year that followed my mother's death, not only was my father riddled with guilt over the fact that he wasn't able to help my mom, but her family began to blame him.

"It's your fault," they told him. "You should have taken better care of Melva."

Soon, the accusations turned to threats. My mother's family would actually come over to our house and threaten my father.

One day, as the arguments were getting heated between my dad and his in-laws, my father stopped, walked away from them, and pulled out his Bible. He sat in the living room with the entire ruckus going on around him and started to read out loud from the book of Psalms 35:

1 Contend, O LORD, with those who contend with me;
   fight against those who fight against me.
2 Take up shield and buckler;
      arise and come to my aid.
3 Brandish spear and javelin
      against those who pursue me.
      Say to my soul,
      "I am your salvation."
4 May those who seek my life
   be disgraced and put to shame;
   may those who plot my ruin
   be turned back in dismay.
5 May they be like chaff before the wind,
      with the angel of the LORD driving them away;
6 may their path be dark and slippery,
      with the angel of the LORD pursuing them.
7 Since they hid their net for me without cause

and without cause dug a pit for me,
[8] may ruin overtake them by surprise—
may the net they hid entangle them,
may they fall into the pit, to their ruin.
[9] Then my soul will rejoice in the LORD
and delight in his salvation.

The more he read, the more things quieted down. As he read, everyone drifted away from him and for that moment, he had some peace. My dad stills calls that a magical moment.

But even though my dad's in-laws stopped all of the attacks on my father, it didn't help; he still felt guilty. Deep down, he knew that what happened wasn't his fault. Deep down, he knew he'd done everything he could have done, but he still felt he was to blame.

The guilt and blame haunted him until a mutual friend of my parents told my dad something he didn't know, and something my dad shared with me when I got older.

"I knew Melva for a long time," their friend told my father. "Even before you did."

"I know that," my father said.

"Well did you know that this wasn't her first attempt at suicide?"

"What are you talking about?" my father asked.

His friend went on to explain that when my mother was in high school, she'd tried to commit suicide then. It had even been reported in the local newspaper.

Those words came as a shock to my father. It was something he hadn't known, something that my mother and her family had kept away from him. But the knowledge did give my father a little relief. My mother had been sick with depression before she'd ever met him. He realized finally that there was absolutely nothing that he could have done to save her. It was just a part of who she was.

From that point, my father did a little bit better. He focused more on moving forward with his life and raising his sons. He never remarried; his focus stayed completely on us, on our education and on our well-being.

He was particularly concerned about our education. When my mother was alive, my parents had decided that we would attend private school because of the major differences in education between the public and private schools in Panama. It was a decision that they made together and even though my mother was gone, my father was going to honor their decision.

But private school was expensive, and financially, it became very difficult for my father. He struggled to meet the school's tuition every year, doing whatever he had to do. If he had to borrow the money, he did. If other bills had to go unpaid, they did. There were times when our phone was cut off or when we had to deal with the embarrassment of our house being lit by candlelight because the electricity was cut off. There were many days when we had no water.

My father could have easily enrolled us in public school to take some of that pressure off. But he didn't. It was all about getting us the best education that would allow us to really advance in life.

So because of my father's dedication, all the years that I attended school in Panama (from the 1st grade till the 6th) I was enrolled in the Instituto Episcopal San Cristobal. Sergio attended the school there from kindergarten until he graduated from high school. Alford was there until the 9th grade. Then he transferred to the same school where my mother used to teach.

But while my father did everything he could to make sure that we went to the school that my mother would have wanted, he didn't fight for me to maintain a relationship with my mother's family. After her death, I didn't spend as much time with my mother's family as I had before she died. The way they treated my father made him not trust them. And he became concerned that my mother's side of the family would try to take me away from him. He wasn't as concerned about them trying that with my brothers; he felt Alford and Sergio were old enough to handle any situation. But he didn't have that same comfort with me since I was so young.

Because of that, I never got to know that side of my family well. Yes, I've talked to them and I've had the opportunity to spend a little time with them since I became an adult. But that family bond was never established and to this day, that hurts me. That is one part of my life that I wish could've been different.

Another thing that changed with my mother's death was what many people would expect - my dad just wasn't the same anymore. The pressure of it all: his guilt, the stress of paying the bills, the burden of carrying all that responsibility alone got to him.

My dad began to drink heavily, though it was mostly on the weekends. There were times when my dad would be so drunk that he would pass out at the bar, and then the owner of the bar would call us. It was the same most of the time - the owner would call us, then Alford would call one of my dad's friends, and his friend would take a taxi to the bar. The friend would pick up my dad, drive my dad's car back home, and we would all have to help my dad from the car all the way to his bed. The whole time, he would be passed out, totally drunk.

Like I said, that was only on the weekends. But even during the week, my father was different. We never really got a chance to see him much or spend time with him. When he came home from work, he locked himself inside his bedroom, and we wouldn't see him until it was time to go to school the next morning. The most time we spent with him was the fifteen minutes that it took when he drove us to school.

Even with all of that, I would say that my father was still a good parent. Whenever we needed him he was there.

My dad was tough, though. He was stern and whenever he spoke, whatever he told us kids to do, we just had to do it - no talking back, no questions asked. All of my friends were a little afraid of him, and used to call my father mean. But I wouldn't call him mean at all. He just had his rules and views, and we had to follow.

Growing up, there were times when I envied my friends because so many of the parents were much more lax in their parenting. It seemed like my friends could do what they wanted, could come and go as they pleased. Some of them were even able to stay out as late as they wanted. Watching them, there were times when I resented my father's rules. Why did I have a curfew? Why did I have to answer to my father when my friends didn't have to answer to theirs?

But now, we've all had a chance to look back on our lives and those same friends who thought my dad was so mean, now say that they wish they had a parent like him.

I guess you don't understand certain things until you are grown. Today, I understand why my father had all those rules and why he wouldn't let me stay out late into the night. He was passing on his beliefs, his morals and his work ethic to me and my brothers.

My brothers and I got along well for the most part. Occasionally we would fight just like any other siblings, but we would get over it, and always ended up playing together. Our age difference was just enough so that we still had a few things in common as kids.

My oldest brother, Alford, was my protector. If anyone messed with me in anyway, they would soon have to answer to him. And usually that wasn't a pretty sight for whoever was involved. There were many situations where he got into physical altercations on my behalf. If that's what older brothers were supposed to do, then he was the model for that role.

Sergio was more like my teacher and he's been that way throughout my entire life. Growing up, he helped me with my homework and was always teaching me anything I needed to learn. Maybe it was because he was closest to my age. Or maybe he felt that was his responsibility, since our mother was gone.

I will always say that I had a good upbringing, but there is no doubt losing my mother was completely devastating. I have forever been deprived of a mother's love. A love that I will never know, but there were many things in my life that made me stronger and prepared me for the many things that were coming in my future.

II.

One Way In And One Way Out

*"It takes courage to live-courage and strength and hope
and humor. And courage and strength and hope and humor
have to be bought and paid for with pain and work and
prayers and tears." -Jerome P. Fleishman*

To know more about me, it's important for me to share a little about the land where I was born - Panama City, Panama. Panama City is the capital of the Republic of Panama, a very small country with an area of only 29,157 square miles. (In comparison, the United States is 3,794,066 square miles). My country is located between Costa Rica and Columbia in Central America, bounded by the Atlantic Ocean to the north and the Pacific Ocean to the south.

Because of its strategic location, Panama became very important for world trade. In school, we all learned about the Panama Canal, a channel that was built to save tremendous time and money for ships to travel from the Atlantic to the Pacific Ocean or vice versa. Instead of traveling around the entire continent of South America, the canal allowed mercantile ships to travel through the continent. Although the French began building the canal in 1881, the United States finished the construction in 1914.

Today, the population of Panama is approximately 3.4 million, with 50% of the country considered Mestizos (mixed European and Indian descent.). The rest of the country is comprised of 22% African decent and Mulattos (one black parent and one white parent), 6.7% Indian, 8.6% Spanish decent, 5.5% Asian, 7.1% are other.

Panama's weather is tropical with a humidity of about 80% year round. We don't have four seasons; we only have two: the dry season from January till May, and the wet season from April to December. With temperatures averaging between 75 to 90 throughout the year, it's no wonder that I never owned a jacket until I moved to the United States.

Pedregalito, a predominantly white or mestizo community, is the middle class neighborhood where I grew up. It was a friendly neighborhood where we were all like family. There was only one street; that meant there was only one way in and one way out. You came in or went out through a narrow street that was lined with identical houses sitting side by side. The only differences between the homes were when the homeowners made additions and renovations.

The street was always filled with the sounds of joy and laughter, since there were so many children around. We were always outside playing some kind of sport. You name it: basketball, soccer, baseball, we played it all.

While we were in the streets, the older teenagers were under the light post playing ping-pong or dominoes with a cooler full of cervezas.

My closest friends were Virgilio, a black kid who lived catty-corner from my house, Calo, an Asian kid who lived a little bit further down the street, and Roni, a mestizo kid who lived almost at the end of the neighborhood.

Virgilio's parents were a little strict so he couldn't play too much. But I could always hang with him right in front of his house.

Calo and I were sports fanatics, playing basketball mostly. And after a good game of basketball, we'd settle in for a long game of Monopoly.

Now when I played with Roni, that was the most interesting. No matter what we did, no matter what games we played, Roni and I usually ended up fighting. We fought, but by the next day we would be hanging out again.

As I said, Pedregalito was a middle class neighborhood, though after my mom passed away, we weren't nearly as well off as the other families. My father worked hard, making sure we always had food and the basic necessities, but that was about it. While most of the kids in the neighborhood had nice clothes, the baddest shoes, and all the latest toys or gadgets, I wore hand me downs from my

21

brothers. And there were times when I had to wear my shoes until there were holes in the soles that led to holes in my socks.

There was a time when I was about eight years old and my shoes were so worn out, there was just no way I could wear them anymore. They were so bad, I couldn't even wear them to go out to play.

My dad promised to bring home a new pair once he got off from work. So, I waited, watching from the window as all my friends were outside playing and having fun.

When my father finally walked through that door with my new shoes, I was so happy! I grabbed the box from him, tore through the paper that covered the shoes, pulled the shoes out of the box, laced them up, then gave my dad a big hug. Now, I could play! I ran out of that house like Carl Lewis coming out of the blocks!

Outside, I did everything. I played a little Hide-N-Go-Seek, a little basketball, a little baseball. Hours passed and when it was finally time to go home, I looked down at my feet and couldn't believe my eyes. The shoes that were brand new just a few hours ago looked as bad as the ones I'd had on before. They had ripped and were covered with holes - after just one evening of playing.

How am I going to tell my dad this? I wondered to myself. My brand new shoes were destroyed.

Slowly, I walked home not knowing what my father was going to say. But when I got into the house and showed my father the shoes, he didn't seem surprised.

"That's okay. I'll get you some new shoes tomorrow."

As he promised, the next night he came home with another pair, but this time, the shoes cost more than $5.00 and were a bit more durable.

That's just one example of how my father tried. He really did the best he could raising three boys by himself. But though he tried, that didn't stop me from feeling poor. It was during Christmas when those feelings of not having enough were especially profound.

Christmas in Panama is a little different than Christmas in the United States. While in the U.S., it's celebrated on the morning of the 25th when kids all over the country wake up to see what Santa Claus left them after he slid down the chimney, there is not a single chimney in Panama!

Our Christmas celebration is very close to the way we celebrate New Year's. On December 24th, adults and kids dress in their best clothes and go to parties that are filled with music, dancing and all kinds of games. When the clock strikes midnight, everyone hugs and kisses, wishing Merry Christmas to one another before the opening of presents begins.

Then, the biggest difference between the U.S. and Panama comes into play. In Panama, everyone in the neighborhood opens their doors and neighbors visit neighbors going from house to house with holiday greetings. In Panama, Christmas is all about family *and* friends.

But while Christmas was always a good time, most years I didn't receive Christmas gifts because my dad just

23

couldn't afford it. But I never let that stop me. I still en-joyed my time as I visited my friends. They always received the toys that I wanted. That was the great thing; I may not have gotten any gifts, but I could always play with the toys that my friends received.

Of course, I had to make up stories whenever anyone asked me what I got for Christmas. Sometimes, I would lie, making up a whole list of wonderful gifts. Other times, I would just change the subject because I knew if I told them the truth, I'd be embarrassed.

In my neighborhood, all it took was for one kid to get a cool gift and before you knew it, all of the kids would have the same item. There was the time when Cutito, a kid whose family was financially well off, got a skateboard, and right after that, all the kids in the neighborhood had one, too. Of course, my dad couldn't afford one for me, but fortunately, Cutito had more than one skateboard and he let me have his old one. I was so happy; I was able to join everyone in the fun. We even built a skateboard ramp and I accumulated plenty of bruises from falling off of it.

But that's how it was in my neighborhood. Everyone looked out for each other, even the kids. And that's why I will always look back on my childhood in Pedregalito with fondness.

Pedregalito is also important to me because it was there, in that tiny neighborhood where I first got my love for the game of basketball. We didn't have a real court to play on, but that didn't stop me and my brothers. We were creative! We used an old bicycle wheel, removed the tires and the spokes, and then hammered it to the roof in the backyard. It wasn't an ideal basketball court, especially since we played on the grass. But hey, it was better than nothing, right? With a beat up ball that one of our friends had, the games were on!

But our basketball fortune shifted when sometime around 1984 we got a real basketball court! It was a gift from a politician who was on a quest to get more votes. So he donated money for our neighborhood basketball court. He purchased everything that was needed for a basketball court: the concrete, the paint, two backboards, two basketball rims, and two basketball nets. Then, he turned the project over to the neighborhood. It was up to us to build it.

Everyone pitched in. It took us two weekends to complete it, but once it was done, we had the real deal. I was so excited to finally have unlimited access to a real basketball court.

My excitement didn't last that long, though. It was great to have a real court to play on, but after the first few weeks, I realized that the new court wasn't going to do me any good. The older kids never let me play because they said I was too young and too little. What was worse was that my own brother was the ringleader. Alford was part of the group that blocked me out. They weren't on the basketball court all the time, just at the best time of the day when the weather was perfect for a basketball game.

I begged and begged and begged for them to let me play. But it didn't matter how many times I said, "Please," their answer was always the same. They refused to the point where all I could do was cry.

I had no choice but to wait for the times when they were off the court, either in the very early morning, or very late in the evening when it was too dark to see. I got used to that and was just grateful that I had some opportunities to play.

But what I wanted most of all was to play with the big guys. Yeah, they were bigger and stronger than me, but I had so much confidence in myself that their size and strength didn't matter. But those big guys were never going to let me play with them.

I bet they'd like to play with me now! What do you think?

Basketball wasn't the only sport that I played, though. Baseball was important to me, too. Not only did we build that basketball court, our neighborhood got together and built a baseball field on a big piece of land that was behind the houses. It wasn't what you would imagine a baseball field to be. There were no manicured grass or fancy bases. It was a dirt field, with bases made of cardboard. We used wooden sticks for bats that we sprayed with silver paint to make the bats look like the professional aluminum ones.

Now while I loved playing baseball and I was good at it, I did have this one little bad habit - I was notorious for throwing the bat wildly after I made contact with the ball.

All the guys playing with me would be ducking and dodging, trying not to get hit by my flying bat.

On this particular day when it was my turn at bat, everyone was shouting, "Don't throw your bat this time!"

Of course, that was my plan. I never wanted to throw my bat. But no matter how much I concentrated, the bat always seemed to get away from me.

"Okay!" I told everyone. "I won't throw it."

But no one believed me. Everyone, including my brothers, moved as far away from me as possible. I'm telling you, there was no one within forty feet of me.

That was okay; I was going to prove them wrong this time. As the pitcher wound up, I gripped my bat. The pitcher tossed the ball, and from that moment, time moved in slow motion.

My eyes were on the ball; it seemed to take forever to get to me. My heart was pounding as the ball floated toward me. Finally, the ball was within my reach, I made contact, and drove that ball all the way into the outfield.

I was excited!

As I took off for first base, I looked back over my shoulder and my bat was sailing through the air like a wild bird. It kept going and going and going until it landed. But it didn't land on the ground. It landed on my brother, Sergio's nose.

An instant later, blood gushed from his nose as fast as tears poured from my eyes. I couldn't believe that I had actually hit someone with the bat. And the worst possible person - my own brother.

I ran over to him. "I'm sorry, Sergio! I'm so sorry."

He glared at me, though he didn't say a word. We got him home, got him cleaned up and thankfully, his nose wasn't broken. And Sergio didn't even make me feel bad about what I'd done.

But from that day, I never threw the bat again. I guess Sergio had to "take one for the team," and I got cured in the process.

***

Although it may seem like it, my life wasn't all fun and games. Of course, I wasn't outside playing all the time. We had to go to school. The schools in Panama were much stricter than the schools in America. There were so many rules, and the one that I had the most trouble adhering to was the rule where I always had to be neat.

That was hard because my school uniform was always sweaty. In the fifth grade, I'd joined the school's basketball team that had been started by Professor Villaneueva. The league was called "mini baloncesto." (Mini basketball, in Spanish). It was called mini because the league hooked lower baskets on top of the regulation ones so that us kids could reach them.

The hoops might have been lower, but that didn't matter to me. It was basketball and I wanted to be the best. So, I practiced whenever I could, especially during lunch time because it would just be my friends and me.

Every day, by the time I finished, I was a sweaty mess. Unfortunately after lunch, we all had to line up and walk past a group of students called "Cuerpo de Orden y Disciplina" or C.O.D. (Body of Order and Discipline.) Their jobs were to make sure that we were neat like we were supposed to be, and they checked all of the kids as we walked by.

After our lunchtime basketball games, my friends and I scrambled to dry our sweat before we reached the security kids. At least three times a week, I was caught not being up to the standards. Each time, I was pulled from the line and taken to the disciplinarian teacher.

Walking over to her classroom felt as if I were walking the green mile. Although none of the kids ever yelled out, I imagined someone shouting, "Here's a dead man walking!"

Finally, I would get in front of her, and with a stern face, she'd assign my punishment - usually detention.

I hated getting detention, but I wasn't willing to give up my lunchtime basketball. So, I was always in trouble.

But I can't just blame basketball for being in trouble. Because for some reason, I was always breaking one rule or another. Take the "No Talking" rule. I couldn't help it. I loved talking to my friends and while the teacher was in the front of the room trying to teach the lesson, I was in the back talking.

One day, my teacher had had enough of me and she called my dad to schedule a parent teacher conference.

My dad didn't like getting phone calls from the school, and when he got home that night, he told me how upset he was. "Now, I'm going to miss a couple of hours of work!"

But like I said before, my father took education seriously. So the next morning, even though he needed to be at work, he was at the school, talking to my teacher about my behavior problems.

The whole class, including me, had to stay outside of the classroom during their conference. Can you imagine how nervous I was? I had no idea what was being said. How much trouble was my teacher going to cause me?

It was a long thirty minutes, but finally that door opened and my father walked out. I searched his face for signs of what my teacher said. I expected my father's face to be filled with anger. But when he looked at me, I didn't see anything different. He looked normal.

I was confused. But then, I thought that maybe my teacher hadn't said anything bad about me. So if she didn't say anything bad, then my dad has nothing to be mad about, I said to myself.

My dad even came over and said, "See you at home." He was smiling, so I was relieved, but just a little. It was hard for me to believe that my teacher had called my father all the way down there and she hadn't said *anything* bad.

"Okay, Daddy," I replied.

All day long, I thought about what my teacher and my father had talked about. And the longer I thought, the more worried I got. By the time 3:00 came around and I was out of school, I was really worried.

I got home at the time I normally did and that was two and a half hours before my dad came home from work.

Usually, after I did my homework, I'd watch television or go outside and play. But on that day, I decided to do something different.

If I'm asleep when my dad comes home, I thought, he won't be able to talk to me about the conference.

So, that's exactly what I did - I went straight to sleep.

The first part of my plan worked! I managed to be sound asleep by the time my father made it home from work. The second part of my plan also worked, but not the way I intended. My dad didn't talk to me about the conference. Instead, he woke me out of my sleep with the sting of a leather belt on my butt.

I shot up in my bed. It took me a few seconds to realize what was going on, but when I did, I knew exactly why I was getting a whipping.

My dad whipped me and didn't stop. He whipped me like I stole something. But the whipping wasn't nearly as bad as the punishment he gave me afterwards.

"And because you can't stop talking in class, I'm taking you off the basketball team."

What? No! He couldn't do that. I was already one of the best players in the league and my team needed me.

In our basketball league, we didn't play against other schools; our school had many teams that represented several school departments and we played each other. So, the bus drivers team played the maintenance team. And the maintenance team played the English department team...and so on.

I was on the maintenance team and all my neighborhood friends who attended my school came to the games and cheered me on. I will never forget how excited my friends were as they screamed, "Pedregalito, Pedregalito, Pedregalito," every time I hit the floor. My friends were all waiting for me to dunk because the baskets were low. But at the time, I couldn't do that - remember, I was only in the fifth grade. Still, I was an exciting player. But according to my father, that was about to come to an end.

Edgil, the head of the maintenance team, found out that my dad was taking me out of basketball because of my misbehavior and he was furious. The day after he found out, he came over to our house and waited outside for a couple of hours for my father to come home. And when my dad walked up, Edgil greeted him.

"Hello, Mr. Daley," he said, holding out his hand for my father to shake it. "I'm Edgil, the head of the maintenance department at Kevin's school."

"Hello," my father replied.

Edgil continued, "Kevin's on my basketball team, and it's my understanding that you're taking him out of basketball."

"Yes," my father nodded, "he's been misbehaving at school, so until he learns how to behave the right way, I'm not allowing him to play."

"But Mr. Daley, Kevin is one of the best kids we have, and I believe he's going to be a great player one day. Is there another punishment that we can come up with?" Edgil anxiously asked.

My father shook his head. "I'm sorry, but that's the punishment I came up with, and it's going to stay like that."

Then my father ended their conversation by going into our house.

I was devastated. If Edgil couldn't convince my father, there was no hope.

Later that evening, the phone rang. When I answered it and found out it was Professor Villanueva, the head of the league, I knew that he had called to talk to my father. I wasn't sure that it was going to help at all, but if anyone could change my father's mind, it was Professor Villanueva.

As I handed the phone to my father, then listened to the one-sided brief conversation, I had hope. I could tell from my dad's responses that Professor Villanueva was pleading my case. But then, I heard my father say, "I'm sorry, but Kevin is still off the team."

Professor Villanueva did not change my father's mind. It really was over. I wasn't going to be playing basketball. Up until that point, I'd always thought my dad was strict, but always fair. Well, he wasn't being fair now. Basketball was important to me, but that didn't seem to matter to my dad.

Even to this day, I get mad thinking about how he stopped me from playing what I loved for the rest of that year! Some say it was the right thing for him to do, I still say it wasn't!

III.

I'm The First In The World

"You can't expect to reap a harvest that you're not willing to plant."
— *Yvonne Pierre*

Those were the good times growing up in Pedregalito. But there was another part of my life outside of that neighborhood that I loved just as much.

Colon, a city about forty-nine miles from Panama City is where my mother and father were born. You may remember that right after my mother passed away, I lived there with my grandmother, but most of my family from both my mother and my father's side lived in Colon.

Colon was not as prosperous as Panama City. In fact, since the 1960s, poverty and unemployment in Colon has been on the rise. Today, the unemployment rate is at a whopping 40%, and those living in poverty is even higher.

But when I used to visit my family, I didn't know any of that. And even if I had known and understood it, none of that would've mattered to me.

While I loved going to Colon to visit all of my relatives: my grandparents, my aunts, uncles and cousins, my cousin, Damian was my favorite. It was probably because we were so close in age; he was just seven months younger than me and he liked doing all the things I liked to do, including playing basketball. Plus, he was the son of my aunt, Ruby. I really liked aunt Ruby because she the only one that would give us a dollar every week as allowance. So, I especially liked going over to their house.

I'm not sure that I ever realized it but, until Damian was seven years old, he, his mom, his older sister, Stefani and his younger brother Dexter, lived in a condemned building. They weren't living there alone; there were seven other families and though everyone had their own apartment, all eight families had to share a single bathroom that was located in the hallway. They also had to share a sink to wash their clothes and dishes. Looking back, that was a terrible way to live.

But the signs of poverty were not just inside that building. There were signs of it on every corner. Damian and I used to walk back and forth between his house and where our grandparents lived. It was just a seven-block walk, but in that short distance, I saw everything: crackheads, prostitutes, lots of stray dogs. People fought right in the middle of the street. The despair was so thick in the air you could feel it.

And you could see it, too. The plumbing throughout the city was in such bad shape, that often the pipes would burst and a current of water carrying everything that you can imagine, flowed through the streets. Walking through the city, I'd have to jump over a gush of water filled with feces, urine, toilet paper...basically anything that was flushed down the toilet. But what was most amazing, was that it was so common, it became normal. No one seemed to notice, no one ever mentioned it.

But even under those conditions I couldn't wait to go to Colon and spend time with Damian. The way they lived didn't bother me; I just loved being with my family.

Ironically, even though the poverty in Colon was so high, I felt poorer in Panama City than I did when I went to visit Colon.

You see, poverty is the great equalizer. In Colon, no one had anything. None of the kids had new clothes or the latest toys or the best gadgets. None of the kids ever had anything that I wanted. But at home in Panama City, the kids there had everything that I wanted.

So, that's another reason why I loved going to Colon; I felt just like everyone else.

Eventually, life got a little better for my cousin, Damian and his family. Around 1983, they moved to a one-bedroom government-owned apartment. In the United States, it would've been called the projects, but whatever the name, their new place was so much better than the run-down building. It was a small apartment, and was especially crowded with four people sleeping in one bedroom (five when I visited.) But this apartment was luxurious compared to where they'd been living. Especially since now, they had their own bathroom inside the apartment. That bathroom alone made it seem like my aunt and my cousins were 'moving on up', just like the Jefferson's.

While I spent a great deal of time with Damian, my grandmother's house was my hangout, too. But it wasn't just the hangout for me. My paternal grandparent's place was the gathering spot for the entire family. Even though it was small, with only two rooms, separated by a kitchen and a bathroom, everyone was always there.

Before I was born, my grandparents only owned one of the rooms in the house and shared the kitchen and the bathroom with a man who owned the other room. A few years later, the man passed away and my grandparents took over both of the rooms, turning one into a living room, and the other, a bedroom.

My grandfather Timothy Daley (we called him Pa) was a carpenter from Kingston, Jamaica. He came to Panama in the early 1940s along with a lot of Caribbean immigrants who'd been hired to help build levees on the Panama Canal. Carpentry was the perfect trade for him; he was a strong man who was good with his hands.

My grandmother, Maude Daley (who we called Ma) was born in Panama and was a cook at a local hospital. Ma was the rock of our family, very loving and very giving. She raised many kids throughout the years, several who weren't even blood relatives. But she raised them as if they were her own.

Ma was a God-fearing woman, who was loved by many. But even though she had lots of friends, what she loved most was having her family around. She loved to laugh (she had a great sense of humor) and she loved to cook. Even though my grandparents didn't have much, when it was dinnertime, Ma found a way to feed everyone who was in that house. My grandfather's friends somehow always found their way to visit him right around dinnertime. Was that a coincidence?

But even though Ma was known for being so kind, she was also the disciplinarian. We couldn't get away with anything, not even a little horseplay.

Once, when my brothers and I were at my grandmother's place, we were so bored that we had to search for something to do, some way to entertain ourselves.

The three of us were sitting in my grandparents' living room and our little cousin, Tonito, was sleeping on the couch, sucking his thumb like he always did.

Alford stared at Tonito for a while and then whispered, "I got an idea."

"What?" Sergio and I asked at the same time.

Alford didn't say a word. He just jumped up, ran into the kitchen and when he came back, he had a bottle of hot sauce in his hands. When he glanced over at Tonito, and then, held up the bottle, Sergio and I got it.

We worked as a team; Sergio gently removed Tonito's thumb from his mouth, moving slowly so he wouldn't awaken him. Then, Alford dabbed hot sauce onto Tonito's thumb, working just as slowly and carefully as Sergio had. It took a few minutes since the prank would only work if Tonito was still asleep.

We gently moved him, just enough so that he would find a way to get comfortable again and stick his thumb right back in his mouth. We sat there, staring, wondering if it was going to work. And a few minutes later, just as we thought, Tonito tossed around a little before he put his thumb back in his mouth. He kinda snuggled into the couch, got comfortable again, and never opened his eyes.

We were already trying hard not to laugh, when all of a sudden, Tonito started licking his thumb, as if it were a piece of chicken. Then, his eyes got real tight before they popped open. And my seven-year-old cousin screamed at the top of his lungs.

We jumped up and tried to run from the scene of our crime, but we couldn't run fast; we were laughing so hard.

When my grandmother found out what happened, she knew the three of us were the culprits. She pronounced us guilty, grabbed the thickest belt and spanked us so hard, none of us could sit in a chair for a week.

Of course, Tonito grew out of sucking his thumb. And now, all these years later, we're able to laugh about it when we see each other. We love getting together and talking about all of those good times.

Staying with my grandmother wasn't all fun and games. The grandkids were responsible for a lot of the errands and chores. Everything from grocery shopping, cleaning the bathroom, washing dishes, and a whole lot more. Like any other kid, I didn't like the chores, but the one that I hated the most was "picking rice".

Rice is a staple of the Panamanian diet, and if it were up to me, I would've eaten rice every day. My grandmother made rice for just about every meal. Since we didn't have a lot of money, we purchased the generic or cheapest brands. But these cheaper bags of rice came at a higher price. The least expensive bags of rice were filled with dirty grains, small rocks, and sometimes even small worms that had to be taken out of the rice before it could be eaten, or even cooked.

So, that was our chore once a week, usually on Saturday or Sunday. The kids had to sit around the dinner table and pick out everything until we made a clean pile of rice. It would take hours, and just when it seemed like we were almost finished, my Auntie Vilma would pour another new batch of dirty rice right in front of us. To make it seem like I worked the hardest, when my cousins weren't looking I would steal some of the rice from their clean pile and put it with mine. It was not hard work, but it was boring and it took so much time.

But once we sat down to a meal and had some of that rice, it was all worth it. My grandmother and aunties could cook and even the part of the rice that wasn't fit for the meal was desirable. We called this part of the rice 'con colon.'

After the rice was cooked and served, some of the rice would stick to the pot - that was con colon. We had to scrape the walls of the pot to get it, but it was crunchy and tasted just as good as the rest of the other rice to us.

We kids loved con colon, either as a late night snack or as extra if we weren't full after we finished dinner. But there wasn't enough to go around, so we fought for it. We had a system, though; the first to yell out in Spanish, "Con colon mio!" would get it. This often created heated fights, but the con colon was so good, it was worth it in the end.

Those were some great days in Colon and whenever it was time to leave, I was always sad. But there was something to look forward to when I went back to Panama City – basketball! My love for the sport was growing and I always looked forward to returning home so that I could get back to playing.

I would get out on that court every day, always trying to get my friends to play with me. Some days they would say yes, but many times, they were too tired to play. That never stopped me. No matter what, every day I dribbled my basketball all the way down to the end of the neighborhood to the court.

My neighbors would hear the sound of the basketball bouncing off the hot concrete street and immediately know it was me, either going to or coming from the court. Nothing could stop me, not even the rain. It could be pouring; I didn't care. There would be no one to play with me. I just didn't care.

Not even holidays got in my way. In fact, shooting hoops on New Year's Eve became a tradition of mine. It started when I was just about nine years old.

It occurred to me that if I shot a basket at the exact stroke of midnight, I'd be the first in the world to make a basket that year!

So as soon as everyone shouted, "Happy New Year!" I grabbed my basketball and ran down to the court.

First, I shot a lay-up, and shouted, "I'm the first in the world to make a lay-up this year."

Next, I shot a jump shot. "I'm the first in the world to make a jump-shot this year."

I did the same thing as I shot a free throw.

Making the first lay-up, jump shot, and free throw became a yearly routine. While everyone else was celebrating, I was honing my basketball skills.

Now obviously, the New Year comes in at different times around the world. So technically, I may not have been the first person in the world. But as a kid, I didn't know that and I was sure that I was the only person in the entire world who was dedicated enough to be practicing during the festivities. I guess that's when my hard work ethic really began.

IV.

Most Likely To Succeed

"When one door closes, another opens; but we often look so long and so regretfully upon the closed door that we do not see the one that has opened for us." -Alexander Graham Bell

Panama is so small that wherever you go, whatever neighborhood you visit, whatever event you attend, you're almost guaranteed to know someone there. And if you think you don't know anyone, someone there certainly knows you.

Before you even make it home, you'll get a call from a friend saying something like, "Hey, I heard you were eating at the restaurant last night," or "I saw you at the store." Some people like that and some don't. I'm one of those people who don't. Actually, I can't stand it at all. For me, the best times are when I can get away to a place where no one knows who I am, where no one knows my name.

Now, that's who I am as adult. As a young boy, I really didn't care. But the dislike I have for that now that I'm grown, is the same way my father felt back then. He felt Panama was beginning to feel too small.

I was twelve years old when my father decided that he'd had enough of living in Panama and he started thinking about moving - to the United States of America.

My father had never been to the United States, but we had family and a few friends living there. So I guess that was a good enough reason for my dad to consider moving there.

But family wasn't the only reason why my dad thought the U.S. might be a good place to live. To my father, the United States was the land of opportunity and my dad decided that he wanted his kids to have a piece of that.

While my father had never been to the U.S., my brothers and I had. We'd spent a summer in New York visiting family, though I was so young that I have no memory of that. As far as I was concerned, when my father announced that he was thinking about moving, I'd never been to the United States either.

The more my dad thought about it, the closer he came to making the final decision to do it. He'd worked for twenty years for the United States Air Force in Panama, so he'd be able to retire and collect the retirement check for the rest of his life. With that check and the salary he would get from a new job in the United States, he figured we could make it.

When I first heard we might be moving to the United States, I had mixed feelings. I had just graduated from the 6th grade and I was reaching the age where I could finally go to the movies with my friends without adult supervision.

Our circle was really tight - there were about twenty of us who'd grown up together, knowing each other since the 1st grade. We were so close, forming a bond like no other. Almost twenty-five years later, we still keep in contact through Facebook and other social media, and whenever I return to Panama, we always have a huge get together. But at that time, of course, I didn't know what the future would hold. All I could think about was leaving my friends, maybe even forever! I was not happy about that at all.

But then, on the other hand, I was really excited about moving because of everything that I'd heard about the U.S., or rather everything that I'd seen on television.

I thought the U.S. was the greatest place on earth! From what I saw on television, there was no poverty anywhere, no trash in the streets, huge houses on every corner, and everyone was friendly.

The one thing I was afraid of was the cold. I'd seen plenty of movies where kids were playing in the snow or people were talking and you could see where their breath met the air as they spoke.

In Panama, that would never happen. You might speak and rain would pour out your mouth, but never would you be able to see your own breath!

And I had certainly never owned a coat in my life. The warmest clothing I had was a long sleeve shirt. And there were times when I wore that and I was burning up.

I didn't know what cold felt like, I didn't know what to expect.

But besides the cold, the rich life, the opportunity, Disneyland - all, the Kardashians...well, maybe not the Kardashians. But all of the other things about the U.S. would be within my reach.

Once my dad made the decision to move to the U.S., he decided to make the trip first, without us, to kind of scout the place. By this time, Alford was twenty and Sergio was seventeen. My father wasn't concerned about them being able to take care of themselves; he was fine with them staying in the house while he was away. But he didn't want my brothers to be responsible for me since I was only twelve. So while my dad was in the U.S., I went to live with my grandmother in Colon.

That was cool with me; Colon was one of my favorite places. Between my grandmother and Damian, I had a great time. Of course, I missed my brothers and father, but I knew my father was doing what he thought was best.

While I was having a good time in Panama, my father went first to New York. His plan was for us to live with some distant family member who had an open basement.

But then my father got to New York, and it was freezing. My father later told us that he had never felt cold like that before in his entire life.

"No!" he said right away. "New York is not the place for us." My father knew that if it was too cold for him, it would definitely be too cold for his sons.

Next up was North Carolina. My aunt Norma was getting married and my dad was giving her away, so it was also a great time to check out that state. But even though it was further south, my dad thought North Carolina had the same problem as New York - too cold!

Next on the list was Los Angeles, California. A childhood friend of my dad's, Waldo, lived there with his family, so that was his third stop in the U.S. Right away, my dad knew L.A. was the place for us. The weather was not exactly the same as Panama's, but it was still good, much better than New York or North Carolina. Snow would never catch us there, so that was a big relief. The palm trees and the beaches were a definite plus. And another positive: the Latino presence was very evident and there were parts of the city that almost (but not quite) felt like home.

My dad rented a very small one-bedroom apartment in Hawthorne, California, a city about ten to fifteen miles southwest of Los Angeles, and on August 3rd, 1989 I finally joined my dad in the land of dreams. Of course, it was very hard to say goodbye to all of my family and friends. Although I knew that good things could happen for us by moving to the United States, a part of me still didn't want to go. Remember, I was twelve, so leaving my friends was a big deal. All I wanted to do was visit the U.S. and then return to Panama to be with my friends again. But I wasn't leaving for just a vacation; this was for good and I didn't know when or if I would ever be back.

What made it even harder for me was that my brothers weren't going with me. Their paperwork hadn't been completed and they wouldn't arrive for a while. So I had to get on that plane by myself, and that made going to the U.S. so difficult.

On the airplane, I looked out of that window as the plane soared into the air and tears rolled down my cheeks. I said goodbye to Panama forever! I cried and cried until I finally fell asleep. It was a long, ten-hour trip with all the connections I had to make, and all I did was eat, sleep, and think about what was ahead for me. There was a mixture of sadness, fear, and excitement inside of me and my anxiety only heightened when the plane was about to land into LAX.

Even through the airplane window, I saw how big Los Angeles was. As we hovered over the city, I could see the huge buildings. And then there were these maze of roads that went on and on; later on, my father told me those were freeways.

Already the city seemed too complicated to me. How was I going to make it in Los Angeles? I didn't know any-one here. I didn't even know if anyone would be my friend. It was all scary and without my brothers, how was I going to make it?

But even with those thoughts in my head, I had a feeling that great things were going to happen for me in this new country. One thing I wasn't afraid of was the language. I spoke some English, though if someone spoke too fast, I would have difficulty understanding. And my accent was very thick, so I wasn't sure if people would be able to understand me. But at least that was better than speaking no English at all.

Once we landed and we exited the aircraft, my eyes opened wide. I had never seen so many people in one place at one time. And the airport itself was so big; I had never seen anything like it.

About an hour after we landed, my dad and I finally reached the apartment in Hawthorne.

The apartment was so tiny, and we just had a few pieces of furniture: two bar stools in the kitchen, and a queen sized bed in the bedroom. That was it. We did have a 32-inch television with only the local channels that my father had sat on top of a cardboard box. But we had to either sit on the floor or on the barstools to watch it.

It was hard at first; my dad and I slept in the same bed and he snored so loudly, it was hard for me to sleep. He sounded like a growling bear searching for food. And he was searching right on my ear.

Being in that little apartment meant that my father and I spent a lot of time together, something that was different for and felt really weird to me. Remember, since my mom died, my dad didn't interact with us that much. Between all the hours he worked, the time he spent out drinking, and then when he was home, spending all of his time in his bedroom, we hardly saw him. And when he was around us, there weren't a lot of hugs, kisses, or even, "I love you"s between us. He didn't spend time helping me with my homework. (My brothers did that.) Nor did he spend time playing basketball or baseball with me. (My friends did that.)

But now that we were in Los Angeles, there was a big difference in him. I didn't know if he saw this move as a chance to better himself as a father, but he was definitely changing in a positive way.

He wasn't drinking nearly as much and he even stopped smoking cigarettes. Thirty years of smoking cigarettes and my dad stopped cold turkey.

But the biggest difference was when he bought me my first basketball not too long after we arrived! I was so excited, not only because it was my favorite sport, but I wasn't used to my father buying me anything. I was so happy about it that I wrote a letter to my brothers in Panama to tell them the big news.

I don't know what's gotten into dad, but he's different. He even bought me a basketball.

My brothers were just as surprised as I was. We'd asked him for things when we were little and after hearing him tell us no so many times, we realized it was much easier on our hearts to not ask, so we just stopped.

Now, I was so happy to have that basketball. I bounced it from the apartment all the way to Hawthorne Memorial Park, a nearby park that had an outside basketball court.

Every day you could hear me bouncing the ball and making my way to the court.

I was always by myself, though, since school hadn't started yet. So, I hadn't made any friends. There were a few kids who lived in the same apartment building, but the maintenance guy had a warning for my father.

"Those boys are up to no good," he said. "They're running with the wrong crowds, so keep your boys away from them!"

To keep me busy and involved, my dad signed me up for a youth basketball league at a YMCA in South Central L.A. I was so excited about this because this was my dad's first time seeing me play basketball. In Panama, even though I was one of the best kids in the school's league, my dad was never able to make it to any of my games.

But now that we were in L.A., he took me to the games and watched. I loved having him there.

Playing in Los Angeles made me up my game. The kids here were quicker, stronger, and had been playing basketball for what seemed like forever. I was no longer the best one on the court, but everyone kept telling me, "You have potential."

At that time, all I would think was, whatever that means.

Those weeks in the summer were great. Yes, I missed Panama, my family and my friends. But I loved the time I spent with my father and the time I got to play basketball.

When school finally rolled around, I was nervous, but ready at the same time. I was eager to make new friends and experience school in the United States.

Waking up that first morning, I had everything planned out. I dressed in plain clothes; no more uniforms, just everyday clothes. But something occurred to me as I looked in my closet. I didn't have very many everyday clothes. Now that I wouldn't be wearing a uniform, what was I going to wear? How was I supposed to wear the same clothes over and over at a new school? It was depressing; I only had enough clothes to maybe last a week and a half.

But I wasn't going to let that fact defeat me. I would just have to get real creative with my rotations. Wear the pants from Monday, with the shirt from Thursday. Then the next day wear the shirt from Monday with the pants from Friday. And I only had one pair of Reeboks to wear with everything. I was going to make it work and hope that no one noticed.

The first week of school wasn't bad. It fact, it was pretty good until the kids started teasing me about my thick accent. There were some words that brought out my accent more than others. Saying Thursday was very tough for some reason. Kids teased me about Thursday and a lot of other words and the teasing really got to me. I got into a few fistfights, and even got suspended from school a couple of times because of the teasing and the fights.

But fighting was all I could do. I didn't know any other way to make the kids stop, until I started making fun of them. After awhile, my jokes started to be funnier than their jokes and all over sudden the teasing toward me stopped.

Once, the teasing stopped, though, I had to deal with another set of kids - the gang members. There were boys trying to pressure me into joining their gang.

Gangs? I didn't even know what a gang was. I was only in junior high school; I didn't want to have to worry about all of these things. To me, school wasn't supposed to be about anything more than learning and creating lifelong friendships.

That's not how it was at Yukon Intermediate Junior High School, though. At Yukon it was mostly about gangs and drugs; Michael Jordan shoes and Starter Jackets. But somehow even with all of this, I managed to stay focused, and except for a few suspensions here and there for defending myself, I was able to even get good grades. I had such high grades that my classmates voted me 'Most Likely to Succeed.' Now, I don't want you to think I was a genius - I wasn't a straight A student by any means. I wasn't even on the honor roll. My grades were just better than average.

It was an honor to be voted 'Most Likely to Succeed' by the other kids. At the time, I couldn't see how that happened. Here I was, a kid from another country who barely spoke English, and everyone thought I was going to be the most successful out of all of us in life. I didn't see it that way, but I guess others did. Others saw in me a greatness that took me awhile to see in myself.

To some that was just a meaningless award in the 8th grade. But to me, that was a defining moment. When I received that validation, when others saw in me what I couldn't see in myself, I knew I was going to make it

I had to make it.

That was when I began to believe in myself more. Just two years in the United States and I was already excelling.

V.

The Eyes Of My Murderer

"It is only at the first encounter that a face makes its full impression on us."- Arthur Schopenhauer

L ife was good - I was doing well academically, and I was growing up. Of course, I had a lot of male friends. My best friend was a boy named Steve. But this was the time when I became interested in girls.

There was this one particular girl, Cindy, who I really liked. Not many boys at school were attracted to her, but for some reason I was. Maybe it was because she wasn't the prettiest, and I didn't feel as if she was out of my league. I don't know why, but I liked her and she liked me.

One day, when we were in class, she came over to me and said, "You should come over to my place after school."

"Really?" I said.

"Yeah, we can talk and hang out. My parents will still be at work."

"Okay," I said. "I'll come over.

But honestly, I was surprised that Cindy invited me over. I mean, yeah, we liked each other. But we hadn't gone out anywhere or anything like that. We just talked at school.

I was so excited and very nervous at the same time. This was the first time a girl had invited me over to her home.

After school, Cindy and I walked to her apartment, along with her little brother. She didn't live that far away from the school, but it felt like the longest walk ever. It seemed like it took an eternity to get there.

Inside her apartment, she sent her brother to his bedroom, and then she took me straight to her bedroom. Now, I was more nervous than excited, but she turned on her television, and we just talked for a while.

All of a sudden - I couldn't really tell you what happened - we ended up laying down on her bed. My heart was already pounding, but when she started to kiss me, I thought my heart was going to pound out of my chest. I had no experience in any of this at all. All I knew was what I'd been told by the guys at school and what I'd seen in movies.

I didn't know what to do. But it seemed like Cindy knew a lot.

As Cindy kept kissing me, I kissed her back. Then, she took her blouse off. When I just laid there, she told me what to do. "Take off your shirt."

She was definitely in control of this whole situation.

So we kissed, and fondled each other, and just when it was about to really heat up, the front door of the apartment opened, and then slammed shut.

My heart that had been beating so fast, just stopped.

"Please tell me that's not your parents," I whispered.

She sat still for a moment as if she were listening and waiting for something to happen.

"It's my father," she said, though I didn't know how she knew that. "He probably got off of work early."

Oh no! I kept screaming that over and over inside. What was I supposed to do? I grabbed my shirt and put it on as fast as I could. Then, I rushed to the window. My plan was to jump out and then run before her father saw me.

But when I looked out, I had forgotten one thing - their apartment was on the fourth floor! I was trapped. There was nowhere for me to go!

"I've got to get out of here," I whispered.

Cindy put her finger up to her lips, telling me to be quiet. And together, we listened to her father talking to her little brother.

"Where's Cindy?" her father asked.

I held my breath.

Her brother said, "She's in her room and there's a boy in there with her."

I knew it for sure then - this was the day I was going to die! If the heart attack I was having didn't kill me, her father definitely would.

"Cindy!" her father shouted.

As she stood and walked out of the bedroom, I ran to the closet.

My thought was that maybe her father would come into her bedroom, look around, not see me, and then think that her little brother had made it all up. I know that it was far-fetched, but I was only in the 8th grade.

And it was a bad idea because just like I thought, her father did come into the bedroom. And he walked straight to closet, opened it up, and found me hiding.

"Come on out, son." His voice was so calm, it scared me even more.

I walked out as slowly as I could, feeling like I was walking to my death.

"What's your name?" he asked.

"Kevin," I replied with my head down. There was no way I could look at him. I didn't want to look into the eyes of my murderer.

There was a moment of silence, and then, "Go home Kevin."

My eyes got so big. That's it? I thought. I couldn't believe it. I didn't say another word. I grabbed my bag and ran out of that apartment as fast as I could. I didn't look back at Cindy's father, and I didn't look back at Cindy.

I was just so happy. I had just been found by a girl's father, in her bedroom, and I was still alive!

I didn't stop running until I was almost home. I may have only been thirteen years old. But I was old enough and smart enough to know that I had dodged a huge bullet that day!

VI.

Wow, This School Is Big

"Do a little more than average and from that point on our progress multiplies itself out of all proportion to the effort put in." -Paul J. Meyer

It was getting close to graduation and the thought of leaving junior high school to go to high school was very scary. At Yukon Intermediate, we heard about everything that was happening at the local high schools. Well, not everything - the rumors were always only about all the negative stuff. We never heard anything good.

The two local high schools were Hawthorne and Leuzinger. There wasn't too much going on at Hawthorne, but Leuzinger always had something happening. I was hoping to go to Hawthorne, but because of my home address I had to attend Leuzinger. That school was known for everything except for learning. From shootings, to gang banging, and drugs, riots and everything else.

A couple of weeks before our 8th grade graduation, we heard about another incident at Leuzinger. Apparently, a Latino girl got into an altercation with a pregnant African-American girl. We didn't know what the altercation was about, but the two of them ended up fighting. Well, that fight led to a school wide riot between African-Americans and Latinos.

When Steve and I heard about the riot, we were even more scared to go to Leuzinger. We were apprehensive that whole summer, worrying about what would happen to us at school. And then when the first day came around, we were really scared.

Steve had called me the day before to see what I would be wearing to school.

"Remember, we can't wear the wrong colors."

By this time, I'd been in Los Angeles long enough to know how important colors were. The wrong color could get us into a lot of trouble, maybe even killed. If you wore red, gang members from the Crips would think you were affiliated with the Bloods. Just seeing red would make the Crips feel disrespected, and they would jump you just for that.

The same thing would happen if you wore blue. Sometimes, the gang members didn't even ask questions to see if you were gang affiliated. They just saw the colors, felt disrespected, and started shooting.

Steve and I made sure that we weren't going to have any red or blue anywhere near us.

That first morning, Steve met me at my apartment so we could walk to school together. It was a long walk to Leuzinger, about two miles; so it would take us about thirty-five minutes.

"Are you ready?" Steve asked me.

I could tell by the look on his face and the way his voice shook a little that he was as scared as I was.

"Yeah," I said. "Let's go."

We had already mapped out our route. We were going to take as many main roads as possible. In case anything was to jump off, we didn't want to be stuck on a side street.

We weren't the only ones on the street. As we walked, we saw all these other kids heading in the same direction, and we checked out everyone carefully to see if they were a gang member before we got too close to them. On the way, we picked up a couple of other kids from Yukon, and I felt a little safer in the larger group.

The whole time I was walking though, I couldn't believe that I was about to enter the doors of Leuzinger. I couldn't imagine what this day was going to bring.

Nothing happened on the way, and I was relieved that we got to the high school safely.

Wow, this school is big, I thought to myself. It was about twice the size of my junior high school. Leuzinger felt like it was spread out - or maybe it was just because the students were spread out. The Black kids were on one side, the White kids on another side, the Asians over here, the Latinos over there. I'd never been to prison, but I'd seen enough movies to know this was just like the segregation that happened in a prison.

Right away, I could see that this was going to be very different from junior high. When I was at Yukon, I had friends from different races, but that wasn't going to happen at Leuzinger. As the days passed, I hardly ever saw different races hanging out together. The only time I did was if members of a sports team were together, or if they were members of the same gang.

Weeks went by and when no one bothered us, Steve and I became less afraid until finally, we were no longer scared of Leuzinger High School. I had figured out that as long as I didn't associate myself with the wrong people, I would keep myself out of harm's way. Now, don't get me wrong, trouble could still come your way, even if you didn't ask for it, but it was less likely if you hung out with the right people.

I even managed to have friends of different races; I had several Mexican friends. But then, one day this Mexican kid (who wasn't even a gang member) got into it with a Black kid who said the Mexican kid was looking at him in a funny way. Can you believe that? Stupid, right?

Well anyway, that one fight turned into a school riot. I'd heard about the riots at Leuzinger and now, I was experiencing it for myself. People were getting hit with bottles, trash cans, anything that you could think of. Some people were even stabbed. It was complete chaos. I had to watch my back and make sure that no one even got close to me.

Police were all over the school and somehow were able to get everything back in order. But even though the riot was over, the danger wasn't. For the next few days, we had to be very careful until the tension died down. First, I had to pretend that I didn't even know my Mexican friends. I didn't like that because I didn't believe in any kind of prejudice. But those were the rules and I had to protect myself.

Then, walking to and from school, we couldn't walk alone because some Mexican gang members, who were still looking for trouble, could catch us. But it wasn't just us - the same was true for the Mexican kids. They had to be just as careful because there were Black gang members looking for any Mexicans they could find.

But even under all those circumstances, I actually started liking Leuzinger, and one of the first things I did was join the freshman basketball team. Being part of that team helped me to stay away from the wrong people, but it also kept me from hanging out with Steve because I was busy with basketball practices and games. I started associating with a group of guys who were into basketball as much as I was. I became good friends with Lenard. He was 6'7" and a really good basketball player. He was just a freshman in high school, but he had already sparked interest from major universities.

Sometimes when we walked home together, I would stop by his house and watch him go through all the college letters he was receiving. I'd stand there as he would glance at the return address and most of the letters he'd toss into the trash can.

"What are you doing?" I asked, the first time I saw him do that.

"They're not from the University of Pittsburgh."

"So what?"

"That's the only school I want to go to. We're from Pittsburgh, so I want to go back there and play in front of my family."

I was impressed with Lenard, but at the same time, I was also a little jealous. I wasn't getting any letters, but as I watched Lenard, that became my goal - to one day have college interest letters of my own.

Even though I didn't have any letters yet, I did have some advice for Lenard.

"I don't think you should throw away the other letters because you never know what could happen."

Lenard wouldn't listen to me, but I knew I was right. See, just about every high school basketball player wants to play Division I basketball. Getting letters from a university was a privilege that didn't happen to many. Getting letters meant that you were one step closer to earning a scholarship. That's what I wanted, a basketball scholarship. But more than wanting the scholarship, I needed it. There was no way I was going to afford to go to a major university without a grant or a scholarship.

But I guess Lenard never really worried about anything like that. It didn't seem like he was concerned about what might happen in the future. Supposed he didn't get a basketball scholarship? Supposed he didn't get in to the University of Pittsburgh.

Maybe he didn't think about any of that because he was so spoiled; he always got everything he wanted. And I mean everything: clothes, shoes, video games, whatever. So maybe he thought that he would get this, too. He'd get into the University of Pittsburgh with a basketball scholarship and all would be well.

Although I didn't agree with his thinking, I understood how he started thinking that way. Lenard lived with his lovely grandmother, Miss Fuller, and not only did she give him everything, but she spoiled his friends, too, taking us all anywhere we needed to go.

She was a real nice lady who treated us well, and invited us to come to her house at any time. We became so close that we didn't call her Miss Fuller for too long. After a while she was Grandma to all of us.

She meant what she said about us being able to come to her house at any time because Donti, one of my other good friends, lived with Lenard and Grandma for a while.

Donti was 5'9, a solid basketball point guard and, just like Lenard, he was able to get just about everything he wanted. Donti's father had passed away and he was collecting the insurance money from his death.

One thing about Donti, though - he had a very short fuse and wouldn't let anyone mess with him. There were many times when he almost found himself in a fight.

Rounding out our click, were Keith and Craig, the twins. They were 6'7" and better football than basketball players, but Keith played on the basketball team. They made us laugh because they fought with each other constantly.

Rhonesia was the only girl in the group. She was a very attractive girl who we all treated like our sister. We used to love to hang out and go to her house when her parents were away. Raiding the refrigerator was our favorite thing to do there and they always had plenty of food.

The thing about it though, was that Rhonesia always found a way to be in trouble, mostly because of gang activity. She only dated gang members. She got into so much trouble, there was even a time when she was on house arrest. She had to wear an ankle bracelet for a few months, and that whole time, she was only allowed to go back and forth to school.

We tried to talk to her about only dating gang members, but that was just her thing.

Lenard, Donti, Keith, Craig, and I spent most of our free time playing basketball. On the weekends we got up as early as 8:00am to go to the courts. If Grandma didn't give us a ride, then we'd walk and sometimes that would take as long as an hour. We played at one gym in the mornings, another gym in the afternoon, and still another one at night. We literally spent all day playing basketball.

And as every day passed, I just kept getting better and better. I was conditioning myself for my future and I didn't even know it.

VII.

There Was No Romantic Music

The discipline you learn and character you build from setting and achieving a goal can be more valuable than the achievement of the goal itself"-Bo Bennet

During my high school years, I had a lot of time to myself. My brothers had moved to California by then and after staying with us for a little while, Alford moved into his own apartment, and Sergio went into the Navy. With my dad working the night shift, going into work around 7pm and usually not coming home until after I had left for school the next morning, I had a lot of free time - and that gave me the opportunity to spend time with girls in the house without having to worry about getting caught.

My life was going so well at that time. School was good, basketball was good and I even had a girlfriend. Tanya and I were both in the tenth grade at Leuzinger. She was very shy, very skinny, and very pretty. Up until that point, I had never had a so-called serious girlfriend. Tanya was my first.

My friends and I were only fifteen years old, but the guys talked about all the sex they were having. I couldn't believe it. I was a virgin and hadn't really thought about having sex. Really, I thought we were kinda young to be doing that, but I never let my friends know that was what I was thinking.

The more my friends talked about having sex, the more I thought about it, and then Tanya and I started talking about it.

"I'm a virgin," Tanya told me the first time I brought it up.

I could've told her that I was a virgin, too, but I didn't want her to know. All I kept saying was that since we were boyfriend and girlfriend, we should do it – especially since everyone else was doing it.

Since my dad wasn't home, Tanya would come over to my house all the time. She had a couple of older sisters who would drive her over; and sometimes, her sister would wait outside in the car, and other times her sister would leave, then come back to pick her up.

We hung out like that for months, not really doing anything. Just hanging out the way fifteen-year-olds were supposed to. But then, my clique just kept talking about sex. And the more they talked, the more I talked about it with Tanya and finally, the pressure got to both of us. We agreed that we were going to do it. So we set the date, and like always, her sister drove her to my house.

I have to tell you, I was so scared. I was scared to the point that my palms were sweaty.

When Tanya walked into our apartment, I tried to play it real cool; it wasn't like this was the first time she'd been at my house. But I could tell that Tanya was nervous, too, because she hardly said a word.

I was feeling like she didn't want to go through with it and so I asked her, "Do you want to do this?"

"Yes," she said.

"Are you sure?"

"Yes. I want to do it as much as you do."

"Okay." Looking back, I wished that she'd changed her mind. But since she didn't, I certainly couldn't be the one to back out.

There was no romantic music, no sexy lingerie, no fragrant body oils, no candles burning, and no rose pedals in the bed that night. As the matter of fact, we didn't even use my bed. We did it right there on the living room floor and it all happened so fast. It was like just a couple of minutes and before I knew it, it was over.

Tanya jumped up, got dressed, and off she went. I was left by myself., with just rug burns to prove what I'd just done.

When Tanya got home and called me, I was so relieved. I wasn't sure if she would ever speak to me again. We talked on the phone all night about what we'd done. It was hard to believe that at fifteen years old, I'd done what should only be done as an adult.

That night I felt like a man, rug burns and all! But as I got older, I realized having sex at fifteen didn't make me a man. I was just another kid who fell to peer pressure and had sex way before I should have. My only excuse was that I knew my friends were having sex, and I didn't want to be left behind.

But then when I thought about it, maybe they weren't. Maybe they were just lying about it the way I had been.

Today, when I speak to kids I tell them to wait. I tell them not to fall to the pressure of their peers the way I did. I tell them to wait until they're adults, wait until they can handle it - physically and emotionally.

Besides my desire to be grown before my time, I pretty much stayed on track. Between school and basketball, I didn't have a lot of time for anything else. But, I couldn't say the same thing about Steve. My best friend got mixed up with the wrong crowd and ended up joining a gang.

When he first told me that he'd joined a gang I thought he was crazy. "Why did you do that?" I asked him.

"Man, they got my back," he responded.

I knew what he meant. With all the problems that were going on at Leuzinger, it was good to have back up. But joining a gang? Did he have to go to that extreme? That was a big deal.

"You should come over there with me," he said. "I'm meeting up with them at the park."

At first I wasn't sure I wanted to do that, but Steve was still my best friend. So, I decided to go, and it wasn't as bad as I thought it would be. Even though I wasn't part of the gang, the guys were cool and friendly. I ended up going to the park with him for several weeks. I went with him so much that one day, one of the gang members approached me.

"It's time to put you on," he said.

I didn't answer right away. I wanted time to think about it, but everyone was standing around watching me. There was no way I could say no. Saying no would make everyone think that I was a punk. And, I was already hanging out with them anyway.

So I stood up and said, "Lets do it!"

"All right," he said.

From that point on everything happened so fast. They took me over to the handball courts section of the park and my heart was beating hard as I followed them. All I kept thinking was, "What did I get myself into?"

But there was nothing I could do at that point. It was too late to back out; backing out would have made things worse.

The gang formed a circle around me. Some of the members I knew, some, I didn't. One of the members that I'd been hanging out with, stepped up. "You have to fight me first." He cracked his knuckles.

I looked into his eyes. He was a little bigger and a little older than me. Over the past weeks, as I'd hung out with him, I'd found out that he'd been a member of the gang for a few years.

As scared as I was, all I said to him was, "C'mon."

He hit me hard on my chin and we started fighting. All that was going through my mind was, "I hope I don't get knocked out." I hit him a couple of times, but he was definitely getting the best out of me. When I thought it was finally over, it got worse.

Two more gang members jumped in. Now I was fighting three guys at the same time. They attacked me, punching me hard and finally, I stopped hitting back. Instead, I used my hands to cover my head, trying to protect myself.

After a few minutes, the punishment came to an end. My body was hurting and I looked like I had said something about Mike Tyson's mother and he caught me! But I must've made it because everyone came over and congratulated me. I was one of them.

I accepted their congratulations, but now as I look back, I think about all of that pain - for what? It doesn't make any kind of good sense today, does it? But back then, I thought it was the best thing that I could've done.

When I told my friend Donti that I had joined a gang, he wasn't happy.

"Why did you do something stupid like that?"

That was the same question I'd asked Steve when he told me that he'd joined. And I answered him the same way Steve answered me.

"Yo, they got my back."

"They got your back? Fool, *we* got your back." His statement took me by surprise and really made me think. The guys on the basketball team did have my back for anything I needed. Maybe if I had thought about that before, I wouldn't have joined the gang. But I'd already been initiated, so I stayed.

Of course, I kept going to school. I had to, I was more afraid of my father than I was of any gang member. But during my free time, I hung out at the park. One day when I was there, Steve and some other guys pulled up in a car they'd just stolen. Now, how did I know it was stolen? Well first of all, none of the guys had a car. And another clue was the screwdriver that was sticking out of the ignition.

"Come on, hop in," Steve shouted out to me.

I jumped right into the backseat. "Where are we going?" I asked curiously.

"We're going to chill in Compton."

So, off we went. Now, in the past, Compton was not a place where we would've hung out. But we weren't in any danger at that moment because there was a gang truce going on. Not that the gangs weren't at war; we were, just not with each other. You see, now, the LAPD was the enemy.

All of this had started a few months earlier after a jury acquitted four Los Angeles Police Department officers who had beaten Rodney King. That led to a six-day, city-wide riot. Right after that, gang leaders from around the city met and agreed to this truce. But like I said, the truce was between us; the war was on with the police.

So, we drove down to Compton, going nowhere in particular. We were just driving up one street, then down the next when the car started sputtering, then stopped right in the middle of the street.

We jumped out, but before we could figure anything out, these guys from a Mexican gang started walking toward us. I could tell they were much older; we were still in high school, but these were grown men.

"What y'all doing here?" one of them asked.

"We just chilling," a couple of us answered at the same time.

"Well y'all in the wrong place to be chilling."

"What do you mean?"

"You're in the wrong neighborhood essay. Don't y'all know the truce is over?"

"Nah, we didn't know that," one of us answered.

"Yeah, it's over, and so y'all better get out of here before we have problems," the spokesperson for the Mexican gang said. Then, he raised his shirt and showed us his gun.

There is only one word to describe me at this point - scared. Here we were, in Compton, with a broken-down car, and seemingly no way out. And right in front of us were these guys who wanted to start trouble.

But someone was looking out for us that day because one of the Mexican gangsters decided to help us fix the car. Maybe he was just a good guy or just in a good mood.

Either way, I didn't care. I was just extremely happy when we were able to get in that car and ride right out of Compton. I had never been so happy to be back home in Hawthorne.

After that incident and a couple of others, being part of the gang didn't make sense to me anymore.

"Why am I putting myself in dangerous situation after dangerous situation for no reason?" I kept asking myself. And, I kept thinking about what Donti had told me, *"Fool, we got your back."*

From that point, I started hanging out more with Donti and the others, and less with Steve and the gang. It wasn't easy at first because every day on the way to school I had to walk by the park where the gang hung out. And of course, I had to do the same thing on the way home.

The first couple of weeks I had to do a lot of running; every day they chased me, trying to beat me up for leaving the gang. But somehow, I always got away.

After a few more weeks passed, I wasn't a concern for the gang anymore. They left me alone; I was free.

That was when I went back to what I loved the most - basketball. Basketball became my outlet from my surroundings. It kept me focused and out of trouble. I played every day, trying to get better. And just when I felt like I was completely dedicated to the sport, I took a hard fall in practice, and banged up my left knee. It hurt pretty bad, but the trip to the doctor made it even worse - the doctor said that I wouldn't be able to play for a few months. A few months! He gave me a long brace and scheduled me to come back to have my knee drained.

Not being able to play basketball was a big concern for me. Now what was I going to do to stay out of trouble? If I had nothing to do after school, I was afraid that I would end up hanging with the gang again. I really didn't want to do that, so I decided to get a job. If I couldn't play, I was going to make some money.

I grabbed a newspaper and started my search. It wasn't easy; no one wanted to hire a high school kid. But then, I ran across an ad for seasonal work at the Del Amo mall. I didn't even know what 'seasonal work' meant, but since they were hiring all ages, I called for an interview.

The next day I showed up at the mall, and to my surprise the job was for an Easter Bunny! Seriously, they wanted me to wear a suit and be the Easter Bunny for the Del Amo Mall. At first, I didn't know what to think. Really? They wanted me to walk around in that costume all day?

But then, they told me that I would earn $6.00 an hour and after that, the decision was easy. I took the job. At the time, the minimum wage was $4.25 an hour. So, I had a really good paying job for a high school kid; it was $1.75 above minimum wage.

I wasn't so sure about the job, wasn't so sure about walking around in a costume all day. But once I started, it became a lot of fun. Of course, some kids were afraid of me because I was a really tall Easter Bunny. (I was over six feet by then.) But the majority loved me and I really started enjoying the feeling of making kids and their parents smile.

Donti, Lenard, and my other friends visited me from time to time. I think they came just to laugh at me in my bunny suit. But it was all in fun and I laughed right along with them.

The only thing was, once the Easter season was over, so was my job. My knee still wasn't healed, and I didn't want to be hanging around, so, it was time to look for a new job.

My brothers had both picked up jobs at Carl's Jr. when they first came to the U.S. and so, when my gig was over at the Del Amo mall, I headed to the Carl's Jr. in the Hawthorne mall. That was even better because I didn't have to catch the bus to get there. It was so close, all I had to do was walk.

The mall is a teenager's heaven. If things got slow at Carl's Jr., I didn't have to worry about being bored. There were always people walking around. So I had the chance to make money and meet girls.

But the thing was no matter how much money I earned or how many girls I met, I missed basketball. I really wanted to play and I started to feel it. Months had passed now, so I went back to my doctor to see if my knee had healed enough for me to play again.

But the doctor didn't tell me what I wanted to hear. In fact, he gave me terrible news. He said that I still wasn't ready to play yet and he couldn't tell me when I would be. That wasn't good enough for me. When I left that doctor's office, I ripped my brace off and never looked back. I got back on that court and it hurt at first, but I played through the pain. With time, it felt better and I guess it healed.

I was back in the swing of things again, playing basketball, hanging out with my friends. And then, I received my report card. My grade point average was good enough to be eligible to play basketball, but the one D in Science didn't make my dad happy.

"You can do better than this," my father said. "I'm taking you out of basketball until you get your grade point average up."

"What? Dad, no. I'll work on my grades, but I love basketball."

I begged, I pleaded, I tried to make all kinds of deals. But nothing worked. To this very day, I know in my heart that my dad made the wrong decision. My grades were good; only one grade had slipped to a D and even that D was still a passing grade.

But I learned my lesson with that. From that point on, I paid attention to my grades. I had to. My grades may have been good enough for the school, they may have been good enough to other people, but my grades weren't good enough for my father. He had his own standards.

As if not letting me play basketball wasn't bad enough, my dad added to my despair when he announced that we were moving to Lakewood, a city that was almost twenty miles away from Hawthorne.

I was upset; moving would be like starting all over. All of my friends lived in Hawthorne and I didn't know anyone in Lakewood.

But my dad was getting serious about his girlfriend and she lived in Lakewood. He wanted to live closer to her.

"Plus, Lakewood is better, it's safer," he told us.

And on my last day of school, my father's words proved to be true. I was so sad as I walked into the gym at Leuzinger to say goodbye to my teammates. But I'd barely been in there for a minute, when there was some kind of commotion.

Two guys were arguing loud and when my friends and I went outside to see what was going on, we saw this black guy who was a known gang member and a Samoan, who was on the football team.

The louder their argument got, the more people gathered around to see what was up.

All of a sudden, the black kid started walking away.

"Where you going, why don't you fight like a man?" the football player yelled at the black guy's back.

"Wait until we get outside," the gang member replied without even turning around. He just kept walking toward the exit of the school.

And the football player was dumb enough to follow him. The crowd followed him, too, and I was one of them.

The Samoan kept talking and the gangster kept saying, "Just wait till we get outside."

As soon as the gangster passed the outside gates, he turned around, pulled out a gun, and fired directly at the Samoan. Everyone, including me, ran and took cover. I didn't know how many shots had been fired, but there were certainly more than one.

When the smoke cleared, the football player laid on the concrete bleeding. He looked as if he were barely alive.

Weeks later I found out that the Samoan had survived, but he was paralyzed from the waist down.

That was exactly what my father was talking about. But even though that's how it was at Leuzinger, I still didn't want to leave. Two years there and I had come to love the school and all of my friends.

But I had no choice. I was forced to enroll in Artesia High School, the closest high school to my new address in Lakewood.

I didn't know much about the school, except that they didn't have as many issues and disciplinary problems as Leuzinger.

On my first day at Artesia High School, I had a big chip on my shoulder. I didn't want to be there and everyone could see my attitude in the way I walked, in the way I talked, and even the expression on my face.

I was in the administrative office registering when I heard shouts coming from the security walkie-talkies, "They're fighting! They're fighting!" The voice coming through the speakers sounded desperate.

I couldn't believe it. This was supposed to be a good school, and there was a fight on my first day.

"Déjà-vu," I thought to myself. It was something that I was used to - a riot between African Americans and Latinos. Seemed to me like all schools had the same problems.

In the end, the riot wasn't as violent nor did it last as long as the riots at Leuzinger. The security guards seemed to be in much more control here.

The school got back in order just in time for me to go to basketball class. I had no idea what kind of basketball team Artesia had, but I expected them to be inferior to the team I'd played on at Leuzinger.

The coach's office was located inside the basketball gym and when I walked up to the door and read the name, I shook my head. "Wayne Merino." I had never heard of him. I knocked on the door and waited for the coach to tell me to come inside.

The coach was sitting behind a desk and reading some papers. He never even looked up when he said, "Come in."

So, I spoke to the top of his head. "Hello, coach, my name is Kevin Daley and I just transferred here from Leuzinger." I'm sure he heard my confidence. Especially when I announced Leuzinger.

"Okay," he said, still keeping his head down. "Change into your practice clothes and I'll talk to you out there."

"Okay." I paused for a moment to see if he would finally at least look at me. When he didn't, I turned to walk out. When I got to the door, he finally raised his head.

When his eyes took in my full height, I could see his shock.

"How tall are you?"

"Six-five."

"Come here, son," he said quickly as he stood up. "Where did you say you transferred from?" he asked with a whole new attitude. Now, he was interested.

"Leuzinger, sir."

"Okay, I'll see you out there." Now, not only was he looking at me, but he was excited.

As I changed my clothes in a corner of the gym, I checked out all the championship banners hanging from the rafters. There were a few California State Championship banners and a whole bunch of league championships.

This school is good at basketball and I didn't even know it, I thought to myself.

The coach came onto the floor, blew his whistle, and we started doing drills. He had us doing drills that I'd never done at Leuzinger. I'd come to this school thinking I was going to be the best player, but there were plenty of guys who could really hoop. Everyone was impressed with my fancy dunks, but that's all I could do well compared to these guys. If I wanted to make this team, I was going to have to work on my game.

I guess Coach Merino saw my potential because at the end of practice, he said, "Welcome to the team, Kevin."

I couldn't wait to tell my dad, and when he came home that night, I met him at the door telling him all about my first day and the basketball team.

"So I guess us moving wasn't that bad, huh?" my dad said.

"Nah." I had to admit that my dad was right and I knew he was glad to see that I was no longer mad about our move from Hawthorne.

At Artesia, I went right to work. Even though the coach believed in me, I knew that I wasn't good enough for this team just yet. I was going to have to work hard if I wanted to get on the playing floor.

From that day, I worked with Coach Merino during lunchtime, during practice, after practice, and on the weekends. I was also blessed to work with well-known coaches like long time NBA assistant coach Tim Grgerich, a personal friend of Coach Merino's. I worked out with former Artesia alums like Ed O'Bannon, who was playing at UCLA at the time and later became the 9th pick in the 1995 NBA draft, and Charles O'Bannon who was also playing at UCLA and had a short stint with the NBA.

Others who would eventually play in the NBA: Avondre Jones, who was playing at USC, and future starts like Jason Kapono, who later played at UCLA and had a nice NBA career winning the three-point contest twice.

So working out with those players helped, but Coach Merino was the best. I always paid close attention to everything the coach said. If he were correcting someone else or giving instructions to another player, I listened. I listened so that I could learn.

It was hard work, but had a lot of fun, too. In my junior year, I began to see real improvements in my game. I even earned a starting spot on the team and later, became team captain. My hard work paid off, and it paid off quickly.

One day after practice, Coach Merino called me into his office. I didn't know what it was about, so as I dressed, I was a little nervous. But then, I stepped into his office, and he handed me two envelopes, both addressed to me. One was from the University of Santa Barbara and the other was from the University of Irvine.

All I could do was stand there for a little while and stare. I was finally getting letters from universities.

There were tears in my eyes when I said, "Thank you," to Coach Merino.

I tucked those envelopes in my pocket, ran all the way home, thinking the whole time how I'd been waiting three years to get letters like Lenard. Once I got home, I dashed up to my bedroom and tore those envelopes open.

Both of the letters were generic letters, very formal, but it was what they said that was important - both universities were interested in me! That was all I needed. Those letters were my motivation. From that day on, I believed that I was capable of earning a college scholarship. That was my new goal and I was on my way.

VIII.

There's A Surprise In There For You

"If you want to live a happy life, tie it to a goal, not people or things."-Albert Einstein

M y junior year was a pretty good year for me and by the time the school year ended, I had a lot of friends. My closest friends were my teammate Donte and Demond, who played basketball and football, and Frank who only played football. We all hung out every day after our practices, most of the time going over to Donte's house to play dominoes. Donte and I became inseparable. Wherever anyone saw me, they knew Donte was somewhere around.

While Donte, Demond and Frank were my good friends, I developed another friendship that was very special to me. Demetrious was on the basketball team, too, but he was a little more serious than my other friends. He really seemed to have his head on straight, but it was because of his mom.

She kept Demetrious focused. Whenever I went over to his house, she would give me books to read, she'd talk to us about our futures and ask me about my plans for college.

There were times when Demetrious was embarrassed when his mom busted out a book and asked us to read a few pages before we went to play basketball. I didn't mind that at all, thought. I didn't have anyone like her in my life and I appreciated her interest in me.

In my senior year, I became even more focused on my goal of earning a college scholarship. With only a year left in high school, I worked with Coach Merino six, sometimes seven days a week. And it all paid off. By the end of my senior year, I performed even better than I did as a junior. I led the team in scoring, I was the MVP of the league, and MVP and an all-tournament selection in all the tournaments that we played in. I was also an honorable mention for the McDonald's All American Team - that's the highest honor a player can get in high school.

But as great as all of those awards were, the one that I was most proud of was the John Wooden Award. I'd won it in my division in high school, and Ed O'Bannon won it for his performance at UCLA. We were two guys from the same high school receiving that prestigious award at the same time, one at the high school level and the other at the collegiate level. I was so honored because I hoped to follow in Ed O'Bannon's footsteps.

The moment was special for Ed O'Bannon, Coach Merino and I because he'd coached both of us. He held his head high and his chest out; he was so proud watching us both accept our awards.

After that, the letters started really coming in from colleges. All of them were Division I schools, though none were major universities. The problem was that I hadn't developed until my junior year, which is considered really late, so many schools still didn't know about me.

The University of Nevada-Reno (UNR) and the University of California at Santa Barbara (UCSB) showed the most interest, so I decided to take school visits to both.

I went to the University of Nevada-Reno first. The university flew me up there and one of the current players from the school met me at the airport. From the moment he led me to the car, the full press was on. From the drive from the airport to the hotel, we just talked about UNR and how good it would be for me to be there.

He dropped me off at one of the best hotels in Reno so that I could change my clothes, before he picked me up and took me to the school.

I felt like a VIP the way the coaches greeted me and told me how much they'd looked forward to meeting me. One of the assistant coaches gave me a full tour of the school. The campus was beautiful - and huge. The buildings were so spread out, I had no idea how many acres the campus covered.

Of course the highlight of the tour for me was the arena. I'd been playing in high school gymnasiums, so the twelve-thousand seat arena was impressive since the largest crowd I'd played in front of was only four-thousand. I stood at the center of that court and looked around at all of the seats. It was hard for me to imagine every seat being filled and me running up and down the court.

I talked to the coaches for a while before I went back to the hotel to wait for another player from the team to pick me up. I was going to hang out with a couple of the players that night.

We went from apartment to apartment giving me a chance to not only meet members of the team, but to see how they were living. They seemed like grown men, living on their own, hanging out, having fun. They were drinking beer and shooting dice. It was all so appealing to me.

I don't know why, but I had been expecting a bunch of college squares, who only cared about basketball. But these guys were into having fun. And lots of it!

After hanging out, drinking, and gambling, we went out to a hip-hop club. A hip-hop club! In Reno of all places! I never expected that. And I really didn't expect to find that the DJ was from Panama, too! This trip was full of surprises.

But the biggest surprise came the next day when my host took me to one of the dorms.

"I've got something for you, KD," he said, calling me KD for the first time.

I couldn't even imagine what it was so I didn't try to guess. But I knew with all the fun I'd had the day before, this was going to be something big.

When we stopped in front of one of the dorm rooms, he motioned for me to open the door. "Just go inside," he said. "There's a surprise in there for you."

"Okay," I answered, filled with excitement, still not having any idea what was behind door number one.

I walked inside, then stopped. Then, I blinked because I couldn't believe what I was seeing. A naked girl was lying in the bed waiting for me. I'd never seen her before in my life, but she was sprawled out there - just waiting for me.

I stood there for a moment asking myself all kinds of questions. Like why? Why would she be willing to do this without even knowing me?

I never found out the answer to that question. All I knew was that this university was trying to do everything possible to get me to sign.

I returned home from my two-day trip, overwhelmed, excited, and sold. There was no way any other university was going to be able to top what I'd experienced in Reno. So, I cancelled my other visit and signed a letter of intent to enroll and play for the University of Nevada-Reno. I was so excited - I had reached yet another one of my goals. I was going to college on a basketball scholarship that paid for all my expenses: tuition, books, room and board, food, everything!

My dad was very proud of me. I was going to be able to continue my education at no expense to him.

That was when I learned the full value of scholarships. Now when I speak to kids, I break it all down for them. I explain that there is no reason for parents to pay for college when there are so many scholarships available. I was lucky enough to earn a scholarship from my passion of basketball and there are many kids who believe that a sport scholarship is the only way to get money for school. So many don't realize that there are academic scholarships, talent scholarships, art scholarships and many more. There are grants that don't have to be paid back. There are so many ways to fund an education. All a student has to do is search and find the right options that are available. All a student has to do is make that his or her goal.

But the first thing I tell a student before I talk about anything else is that grades matter. No matter what you want to be or where you want to go, it's important to start with first things first. And the first thing - get good grades.

IX.

That Was Not My Life

"Peer pressure has many redeeming qualities. It is the pressure of our peers, after all, that gives us the support to try things we otherwise wouldn't have." - Bill Treasurer

I was finally at the University of Nevada-Reno and I couldn't believe it. Even though I'd been to the campus, it seemed even bigger than before. This time, I was able to take in the beauty of Reno, especially the skyline with those huge, beautiful snow-capped mountains. They were far away, but the sky was so clear that they seemed close enough to touch.

Being in Nevada had me on cloud nine and I was full of confidence. This marks my independence, I thought. I no longer have to answer to anyone; I'm in full control of my life.

I guess my thoughts were the same as my father's. Because I found out that just hours after I left for college, he turned my old bedroom into an office. Seems like that was his independence also.

I was one of two freshmen coming onto the basket-ball team. There were other new players as well, but they were junior college transfers with experience playing college ball.

The coaching staff decided to "redshirt" the other freshman, who happened to be my roommate, Tommy. Redshirting meant that Tommy wouldn't play for a year, but he wouldn't lose any eligibility. So with Tommy red-shirted, that meant that I was the youngest active player on the team.

As expected, I didn't play much that year, only about five to ten minutes a game. But hey, most freshman don't even get that, so I was happy with the time I got. And anyway, I was having too much fun celebrating my first time living on my own.

Like I said, Tommy was my roommate and he was also from California - Sherman Oaks. We stayed in a small dorm room that had one common area that served as the bedroom/living room/studying area. In that small space, there was never any privacy. If you wanted privacy, you had to go to the bathroom or leave the room altogether.

Tommy was my complete opposite. He was very quiet, kind of shy, didn't care much for partying, and girls were not his priority. Every time I walked into our room, his head was in a book.

That was not my life. I was living for the parties, drinking regularly, and trying to get every pretty girl on campus. I was hanging with all of my peers, doing everything that the other guys were doing. Studying was my last priority.

Sometimes after a late night of partying, I would return to the room with a girl and Tommy would still be awake, studying. I tried to set him up a couple of times, bringing a friend of the girl that I was with to the room with us. But Tommy never wanted to have anything to do with that. I didn't understand him. To me, college was all about partying and girls.

I began to wonder if Tommy was even into girls. It seemed to me that if you weren't partying and hanging with girls all the time, something had to be wrong with you. But no matter what I said or what I did to get Tommy to be more like me, he never changed. His mind was set on his books.

Of course now when I look back on those days, I have wisdom. And I know that Tommy was the one who had his priorities straight. His focus was on the reason he entered college - his education. He was the one who had everything right; I had it wrong. All that time I thought he needed to be more like me, and I was the one who needed to be like him. He was the one who said no and who was focused. I lost focus. I lost it early and I lost it fast. I could blame some of it on peer pressure because that pressure to fit in was all around me, all the time.

An example of that kind of pressure came down on me one day when a couple of us were riding back from practice in one of my teammate's SUV. One of the guys pulled out a blunt, took a puff, and then passed it around. Up to that point, I had managed to stay away from marijuana and any other drugs. I knew guys in high school who smoked, but I never did - not even when I was in the gang. Out of curiosity, I had once taken a couple of puffs of a cigarette, but no more than that.

But sitting in that car, on that day, I couldn't say no.

The guy sitting next to me, handed me the joint. "You smoke, right?"

Without hesitation, I nodded, grabbed the blunt, and inhaled as if it was a cigarette. Big mistake! That thick, warm smoke flooded my lungs, and I started coughing hard and loud. Then, I started spitting. I couldn't stop - coughing and spitting. Spitting and coughing.

Everyone in the truck cracked up, laughing at me.

"Maaaan, I thought you said you smoked," the guy who'd handed me the blunt, said.

"I do," I said in between my coughs. I felt like the life was being choked out of me. After I regained my composure, I said, "This is just a type that I'm not used to."

I made it through that blunt, and after that, I smoked every chance I got. I smoked with the basketball players, the football players, and other athletes. I smoked with guys and I smoked with girls. And not just athletes, I smoked with non-athletes, too. I smoked with anyone who smoked and it seemed like everybody was doing it. Smoking marijuana not only helped me to fit in, I also liked the way it made me feel.

But then after a few weeks, I saw a decline in my basketball performance. It didn't take long for my stamina to go down, and honestly, I was losing my motivation for the game, the game that I loved, the game that gave me confidence, the game that got me to the University of Nevada-Reno.

Think about that - throughout all of these years, nothing had ever been able to break my focus or motivation for basketball, but in just a matter of weeks, marijuana did it.

I was smart enough to know I couldn't let that happen. It was that loss of motivation that finally made me stop. I stopped smoking cold and whenever someone asked if I wanted to smoke, I simply said, "No."

I redirected my attention back to basketball, and even with my lack of focus and the trials of becoming acclimated to college, I ended up doing fairly well as a freshman; especially considering the little playing time that I was given. By the end of the season, we'd won twenty-one and lost ten games - not a bad record.

Now that I'd completed my freshman year in college, I was full of confidence when I returned to Los Angeles that summer and played in the summer leagues. The best league for college players was the "Say No Classics" and I was on a very good team with great players that included UCLA's point guard, Cameron Dollar. Two seasons prior, he'd won a national championship with UCLA where he was a key player in the championship game when the starting point guard, Tyus Edney went down with an injury and Cameron had to come save the day. And Cameron did that. They won the NCAA national championship, although that was the last one of the eleven championships that UCLA would earn.

I was playing so well that summer that Cameron, without my knowledge, told UCLA's head coach, Jim Harrick about me. Cameron really felt that my skills were so good, that I should be playing for UCLA.

When Jim Harrick came to one of the games to watch me, I didn't even know he was there at first. I knew something was up, though, when Cameron whispered in my ear, "Play well today, 'cause you could end up at UCLA."

I didn't know what he was talking about, but I said to myself, UCLA? Wow, that's the cream of the crop.

Cameron motivated me and I played a great game with plenty of spectacular dunks. That had become my signature - my dunks. It was such a regular routine for me that one of the league's coordinators had given me the nickname "The King of Tip Jams".

After the game, I found out that Jim Harrick was there and I was excited. I called Coach Merino and told him about the game and Jim Harrick.

"I know Jim," Coach Merino said. "I'll give him a call."

There were two things I knew for sure - that Coach Merino really knew Jim Harrick because Ed and Charles O'Bannon had played at UCLA. And I knew that if Coach gave me his word that he would call, he would. And he did.

A few weeks later, Coach Merino and I went to UCLA to meet with Coach Harrick. I couldn't believe that I was actually going to meet with this great coach and I'm telling you, I was so nervous. And my nerves got me thinking. As I sat there waiting to talk to him, I began to think about my playing and started to second-guess my skills. Was I good enough? Could I play on a team as prestigious as UCLA?

But I pushed those thoughts aside. If Coach Harrick thought enough of me to have me come to UCLA for this visit, then, I had to be good enough to be a UCLA Bruin.

Coach Harrick greeted us, and then he led us into his office. As I sat in front of his desk with Coach Merino beside me, I had no idea what Coach Harrick was saying. His mouth was moving, but I didn't hear a thing. My thoughts had clogged my ears. I couldn't stop thinking of the possibility of becoming a UCLA Bruin.

I had heard that when UCLA had a new recruit come in, they always set up a pretty girl to show the recruit around campus. But in my case, Coach Harrick walked me around himself. He wasn't the pretty girl that I expected, but by him giving me the tour of the campus, it showed that he was very serious about me.

We chatted as we walked and he pointed out all the buildings. It was really a beautiful campus with, of course, that great Los Angeles weather. And not only that, I would be transferring from a mid-major university to a basketball powerhouse, full of basketball tradition. What was so unique about this move was that most players who transferred from one university to another, did it the opposite way. Many left the powerhouse schools where they weren't getting enough playing time to go to a lower caliber school so they could be on the court.

Honestly with this move, playing time was something that I had to consider. I'd have more playing time if I stayed at Reno. And, I was happy there. But this was UCLA. This school was so respected, I would be playing in the city where I went to high school. I'd be able to play in front of my family, friends and fans. This was too big an opportunity. In the end, I had to take it.

But accepting the offer was just one part of this deal; I had to call my coach at the University of Nevada-Reno and let him know my decision. As difficult as it was to do, I wanted him to hear it from me and no one else. Yes, it was going to be hard to talk to him, but it was the right thing for me to do.

Just like I imagined, it wasn't an easy conversation. He didn't want me to go and tried to talk me out of it. But, no matter what he said, I knew the coach was aware this was too good an opportunity for me to pass up. He knew that I had to go play at UCLA.

So at the beginning of the next semester, I became a UCLA Bruin! Because of the National Collegiate Athletic

Association's (NCAA) rule, I had to redshirt for a year. I could practice and do everything else with the team; I just couldn't play in the games. To many people, that probably sounded like a foolish thing for me to do - to sit out at UCLA when I could have been playing at University of Nevada-Reno. But in actuality, this was a very smart move for me to make.

Think about it, for a year all I did was practice, learn the system, and improve my skills. After that year was over, I was still eligible to play for the next three years. I was actually gaining a full year of play.

Now don't get me wrong; it wasn't easy to sit out. Because at the time, all I could see was all the work I was putting in: conditioning, practicing, working with weights two days a week, going to classes and study hall, doing everything to be at the top of my game and at the top of my class. And after all of that, I had to sit on the bench. The reward for the hard work was supposed to be the game. I was not being rewarded.

There was one game, though, where I was able to play - the "Fan Day" game. That was the day when the fans and the media had a chance to meet the men and women's basketball teams.

During Fan Day, we played against each other, had a dunking contest, a three-point contest, and played a few other games. We also had a couple of events with the women's team.

That day, I won the dunk contest and had several spectacular dunks during the actual game. After the game, when we were signing autographs, the fans were all over me.

"Those dunks were great," many of them said.

Others said, "We can't wait to see you play!"

That made me feel good. Made me feel like I was putting in all of that work for a reason.

After Fan Day, I went right back to practicing and the

practices at UCLA were a lot tougher than they were at Nevada. At UCLA, they were more intense and the players were more skilled. Coach Harrick often yelled at me for one reason or another, but I didn't mind. A couple of the players told me that coach's yelling was a good thing. You only had to worry when the coach didn't say anything to you. Actually, Harrick's style was very similar to Coach Merino's coaching method.

But then, one day the world at UCLA changed. The day had started out as normal as any other: I went to class in the morning, I hung out on Bruin Walk (the place on campus where students hang out the most), I stayed there and talked to people until the late afternoon, and then, I headed over to Pauley Pavilion for basketball practice. Inside the locker room, we all joked around as usual as we dressed for practice, then went out to the court. We played around, practiced a little, waiting for the coaches to come. Usually, the coaches walked down the steps toward the court together and that was the official beginning of practice.

Like every other day, the coaches came down the steps, but something was odd; Coach Harrick wasn't with them. That was really strange because I couldn't recall one practice that Coach Harrick missed.

The coaches told us to all sit down and then one of them announced, "Coach Harrick is no longer with us. He's been fired."

We sat there stunned, in dead silence as the assistant coach told us that UCLA's Athletic Director had fired Coach Harrick for supposedly lying on an expense report about the number of current players that attended a dinner with future recruits. Apparently the NCAA had a rule that you could only have a certain number of current players during recruiting visits. If you had more players than allowed, the NCAA called that an improper extra benefit for those extra players. It seemed like a stupid rule, if you asked me. But I guess a rule is a rule.

Of course, the mood was really somber during practice and right after, all the players and coaching staff went over to Coach Harrick's condo which was not too far from the university.

When he opened the door, Coach Harrick grinned. He loved us and we wanted to show him that we all loved him. Hanging out that night just talking and having fun made it a great evening, but it got emotional at the end. When it was time to leave, it hit us again. Coach Harrick wasn't going to be our coach anymore and it was as if we were hearing the news of him being fired for the first time.

Walking away from Coach Harrick that night made me think about my being at UCLA without him. I still felt that I had a bright future there - at least that's what I was hoping.

But then, Coach Lavin, who was the assistant coach, was given the interim head-coaching job and while some of the players were very excited about Coach Lavin being the head coach, I wasn't. I had a real bad feeling about the whole thing, but I never said anything to anyone.

It turned out that, unfortunately, I was the one who was right.

Kevin Daley

X.

You Just Keep Doing What You Doing

"Nothing is predestined: The obstacle of your past can become the gateways that lead to new beginnings"- Ralph Blum

At the end of that season, two things happened: I was now eligible to play, and Coach Lavin was awarded the permanent head coaching position.

Most of the players were so excited about that, but like I said before, I wasn't. My thoughts about Coach Lavin were that he was a great assistant coach because he was a great motivator. He was real good friends with the players, and he always knew the right things to say, but I didn't think he was fit to be head coach. He didn't know enough about the strategies of the game.

After we played a few games, those same players who were so excited about Lavin, didn't feel the same way anymore. More and more, the players would sit around and talk about just how unhappy they all were with him.

When the new season started, after we'd played a couple of games, I realized that I wasn't getting the amount of playing time that I felt I deserved. Yes, we had new big-time recruits like Baron Davis and Earl Watson, but neither of them played my position (I was a small forward) and I felt that I had something to offer the team.

Coach Lavin wouldn't put me in the games until it was meaningless. I didn't get to play until we were either down by a lot, or winning by a lot. And in whichever scenario, he only put me in where there were less than two minutes in the game.

During those meaningless minutes, I played with so much anger. I was angry because I should have been play-ing when it counted. I had too much talent to only be in the game when it was already out of reach.

I made the most out of those minutes, though. I used that playing time to do my best. And I did my best to try to kill my opponent.

I wasn't the only one who felt I should have been playing more; several sports writers wrote newspaper articles saying that I should have been getting more playing time.

But I had hope; I was absolutely sure that things would turn around for me during our biggest game of the year - we were playing the USC Trojans, our major rivals. That was always a big game between the two schools, no matter the sport. The schools were only twelve miles apart, and there had always been such rivalry, such hostility between the two.

The game meant even more to me because my girlfriend played on USC's women's basketball team. She and I always had verbal battles, bragging about our schools. This was the perfect opportunity for me to shut her up!

I got ready for the game the same way I always did, with my headphones blasting in my ears, dancing around so that I could get loose, and joking with my teammates. I was in a wonderful mood. Why wouldn't I be? This was the big game, it was sold out, it was going to be televised, and Coach Lavin was certainly going to let me play. Then, all of my friends and family would get to see me play.

From the very beginning of the game, it was a battle. It was so close, and the lead kept changing. I sat on the bench patiently, anxiously waiting for my turn. I knew it was coming. This game was too important and I could play a valuable role.

Of course I cheered my team on from the bench, but the whole time, I kept my eyes on the clock.

"Man, I can't wait to get in there and play," I kept saying to myself.

Half time came and I still hadn't been taken off the bench. But, I was still optimistic. There was still the second half. Well, the second half came, but my turn never did. Coach Lavin didn't put me in the game at all.

And not only that - we lost!

We were quiet and pissed in the locker room, and I was still feeling that way when I went back to my girlfriend's apartment that night. Yes, I was very upset about the loss, but my real anger came from not playing in the game at all. How could Coach Lavin do that to me? Why was he treating me like a scrub?

I didn't want to talk about it, though. No matter how many times my girlfriend asked me, I didn't want to talk to her, or anyone.

"I just want to take a shower," I said, tossing my bag onto the bed and going into the bathroom.

Inside the tub, I stood under the showerhead, letting the water hit my face. I stood there with the water drenching me, and all kinds of thoughts going through my head.

All over sudden I dropped to my knees and just stayed that way, with the water still pulsating over me. Water drenched my face, and it took a couple of minutes for me to realize that there were tears mixing with the shower's water.

I didn't cry often, but that night I stayed in the tub, on my knees, for at least twenty minutes crying like a baby. I just couldn't understand why the coach was doing this to me. I had worked so hard, but it was clearly didn't matter. This was not how I envisioned my years of playing ball at UCLA.

Finally, I stood up, turned off the water, dried myself off and made up my mind about what I was going to do. The next day I called Coach Lavin and got through to him right away.

"Coach, can I come in and talk to you?"

"Sure," he said. "Come in around noon."

I was glad I had an early appointment because I didn't want to wait all day. I had a lot on my mind and I already knew what I needed to say.

I walked into his office, and he sat behind his desk, with his hair slicked back and a huge smile on his face. "What can I do for you, KD?"

I smiled, too, but inside, I wasn't smiling at all. I was mad, hurt, in pain, and embarrassed by the amount of time I was spending on the bench.

One thing I didn't want to do, though, was let my emotions get the best of me. I wanted the coach to know how I felt, but I wanted to do it in a controlled, mature way. If I had a bad attitude, that would give Coach a reason to say 'That's why you're not playing.'

So I took a deep breath and said, "Coach, I want to talk about my playing time. I really feel that I'm doing everything I need to do to play in the games, but obviously that is not the case because you're not playing me. Can you please just let me know what I need to work on or what I need to do to get more playing time?"

Coach Lavin leaned forward in his seat and looked me straight in my eyes. "Kevin, you're doing everything you need to do. Don't worry; in the next few games you'll be playing a lot more. You just keep doing what you're doing."

Wow! I couldn't believe what I was hearing. He actually told me what I wanted to hear - that I would be playing more. That was a quick meeting and I left his office feeling like a new man. That week in practice, I worked harder than ever.

But then a couple of days later, the team received bad news. Two of our key starters were suspended for violating the substance abuse rules. And one of the players was a small forward - my position.

I wasn't thinking about myself, though. I was thinking about my team and I wasn't happy about the suspensions. Especially since I didn't think the players received the support they should have from one of the assistant coaches. In my opinion, he didn't back up our players at all. In fact, this assistant coach even told us how disappointed he was with the players and that he couldn't believe they would do this to the team.

It was hard for me to believe that coach was saying that. Somehow, he'd forgotten the similar situation he'd found himself in during his basketball career. He, too, had battled substance abuse.

To me, that man was a hypocrite. I guess he didn't know that we knew about his past. I wasn't sure if the other players knew, but I knew.

So I wasn't happy about anything that was going on with the suspended players. But there was one thing about it - this had to mean more playing time for me. And Coach Lavin had just made me that promise. So I had to admit that I was looking forward to my opportunity.

My opportunity did come, but it didn't look the way that I expected.

We were playing in the Alaska shootout. It was a nationally televised game and we were playing the great North Carolina team. Every college basketball fan was watching the game, especially since future NBA stars like Vince Carter and Antawn Jamison were playing.

By the end of the first quarter, we were losing, and I was still sitting on the bench. But then in the second quarter, Coach Lavin called for me to go into the game.

I jumped off the bench excited! Finally I was going to get my chance to play in the first half of the game! I was going to play when the game hadn't yet been decided!

Even though I was thrilled, I had to control my emotions. I was determined to make the best of this time. I had to show Coach that he'd made the right decision.

The role of a player coming off the bench is to enter the game with lots of energy, and then try to do as many positive things to help turn the game around.

So, that is exactly what I did. We were on offense and right away, the ball came my way. As fast as I could, I drove to the basket. Just inches from the basket, Vince Carter fouled me. As soon as I felt the contact, I shot the ball. It hit the backboard and went in, and one!

My teammates cheered as I went to the free-throw line. Even though I could hear the cheers, my mind was in full concentration mode. I dribbled the ball my usual four times at the free-throw line, kept my eyes on the basket, and shot the ball with a perfect follow through. The only sound that filled the gym was the nice sound of *swoosh* as the ball went through the net.

There were cheers, but that wasn't all I heard. I also heard the buzzer, indicating it was time for a substitution.

It never occurred to me that someone was coming into the game for me, but when my teammate tapped me on my shoulder, I couldn't believe it. Why would the coach be taking me out right then?

I'd just helped the team. I'd scored a basket and made the free throw. I'd done exactly what I was supposed to do coming into the game.

But none of that mattered. The coach was taking me out.

As I sat on the bench, all I could think was that this was unbelievable. I was in the game for such a short time, I didn't even get a chance to do anything wrong. And I never went back in.

On the whole trip home from Alaska to Los Angeles, I thought about that game. I thought about what Coach Lavin had said to me and how he'd promised me more playing time. But he hadn't kept his word and I didn't understand why not. Why did Coach Lavin lie to my face? Why did he put me in the game and then, snatch me right out, even though I'd made something happen? By the time I got home, I was pretty sure that I'd figured at least part of it out - the coach had put me in, thinking that I wouldn't do well. And then, when I did, he decided to take me out before I had a chance to do more.

I'd heard rumors that Coach Lavin's friendship with Coach Harrick had gone bad after Coach Harrick was fired. Maybe that was it. Maybe Coach Lavin was taking it out on me because I was the player that Coach Harrick really liked. The more I thought about it, the more that I was sure that was it.

Over the next few days, I really thought about it and I was sure that my conclusion was correct. But I never said a word to anyone about how I was feeling. What would I say anyway? And who could I talk to about this? Since I didn't have the answer to either question, I just kept my mouth shut.

The only good thing that happened to me during that time was that one night, Lenard and Donti, my friends from Leuzinger High School came to one of the games. I was so glad to see them, even if they didn't get a chance to see me in action. Just coming to a game at UCLA was exciting enough for them.

After the game, we hung out in the locker room and I was glad to have that opportunity because I had heard that Lenard was out there doing things that he shouldn't have been doing.

It was sad; Lenard was supposed to be the superstar among us, but things hadn't gone well for him. He never played for a Division I school after high school because his grades weren't good enough. So, he ended up at Fresno City College, a junior college, and I think that's when all his problems began. It was during his time at Fresno when Lenard turned to the streets.

I'd heard all kinds of negative rumors about Lenard, and I couldn't believe this was happening to the one everyone thought was going to be the superstar, to the one who was getting letters from colleges when he was only a freshman in high school. I wanted to do everything that I could to encourage my friend.

"Man, you need to stay away from all of that," I told him after we caught up on what he'd been doing.

"Yeah, I know. But what else am I gonna do?"

"Look, if you stay out of trouble, I'll make sure that you get a spot on my summer league team."

That seemed to surprise him. "Really?"

I nodded and to seal the deal, I gave Lenard a couple of pairs of my shoes and some t-shirts and shorts. "Just promise to stay out of trouble."

"I will, man, I will. I promise."

With all that was on my mind, I was glad to have that bright spot in my life. It had been so good to see Lenard and Donti and I was looking forward to hanging out with them more over the summer.

But while seeing my old friends felt good, I still had to deal with what was going on with Coach Lavin. No matter what, he still wasn't giving me any more playing time.

One day when I was in my dorm room, I got a call from Coach Merino. That wasn't so unusual; he called occasionally to check up on me. But this time, he called with a purpose.

"Jim Harrick wants to speak with you," Coach Merino said. "He wants us to meet him at his son's house in Pasadena."

I was shocked that Coach Harrick wanted to talk to me, especially since he no longer had any obligation to me. He had landed a job at the University of Rhode Island, and I so wished that I could go play for him. Of course I could, but the NCAA rules that were in place didn't benefit me doing that.

We arranged to meet a few days later, but the whole time before the meeting, I wondered why in the world Coach Harrick wanted to talk to me. On the day of the meeting, Coach Merino picked me up from campus, and together, we went to Pasadena.

For most of the drive over, I stayed quiet; there was a lot going through my mind

When we got to Pasadena, Coach Harrick greeted us like old friends, invited us inside, and then, he sat across from me and Coach Merino.

As Coach Harrick sat back in a Lazy-Boy type chair, he calmly told me that he had watched the North Carolina game. "I feel bad about what's happening to you. I think Lavin isn't playing you because of what happened between us."

I'd been right! I was so relieved to hear him say that because that meant that what I suspected was true. All this time I'd been searching for answers, all this time, I had my suspicions, and now Coach Harrick confirmed it.

But as relieved as I was, I was also angry. I had nothing to do with their friendship falling apart, yet Coach Lavin was punishing me. And for what? This was my career, not Coach Harrick's.

Then, Coach Harrick told me the truth. "If you want to make basketball your career, you're going to have to leave UCLA and go somewhere where they'll let you play. You're not going to get a job sitting on the bench."

For hours after I left Coach Harrick, his words reverberated through my mind. I loved UCLA and I couldn't imagine leaving after being there for two years. But I had to make a decision.

The good thing about it, though -I had all summer to think about it.

XI.

I Just Couldn't Believe It

A gentleman can withstand hardships; it is only the small man who, when submitted to them, is swept off his feet."-Confucius

F or the summer, I got an apartment with two of my teammates, Rico Hines and Baron Davis. I felt so out of place because I was living with them and I had no money. They had everything they needed and more. Baron's room was fully furnished with a huge California king size bed and he drove a brand new Ford Expedition. Rico's stuff wasn't as extravagant as Baron's, but it was much better than anything I had. In my room all I had was a television sitting on top of a cardboard box and a futon bed that my girlfriend had planned to throw away, but instead gave it to me. Even my car was beat-up. I was driving an old 1989 Chrysler Le Baron that I had saved up for.

Although I had a full scholarship, I still had to get a small student loan during the summer to cover my expenses. The loan was just enough to cover my share of the rent. Everything else I had to figure out on my own. Each morning, I had to search for pocket change to buy two .99 cents chicken sandwiches at Jack 'N the Box. That was my breakfast, and I usually wouldn't eat lunch - I couldn't afford to. For dinner, I bought something cheap and simple from the grocery store like Hamburger Helper. Every day was a challenge to figure out how I was going to eat.

But not having money wasn't the only bad thing in my life. A major blow came when I found out that Lenard had been arrested for trying to rob a bank. And when the police were trying to arrest him, they shot him, leaving him paralyzed from the waist down.

I just couldn't believe it! I was mad at the police and I was mad at Lenard. It had just been a few weeks since I'd seen him and Donti. Obviously, he hadn't kept his promise.

In the morning newspaper on the day after the shooting, there was a picture of Lenard lying on the ground after being shot. I stared at the picture for a long time; he was lying there with a pair of shoes that I'd given him the day he promised he would stay out of trouble.

After hearing the news, I spent as much time as I could with Donti and Rhonesia. We needed each other because all of us were taking the news of Lenard hard. Every day, I drove back to Hawthorne to hang out with them. We were each other's support as we dealt with the fact that not only was Lenard never going to walk again, but he was going prison for twelve years. The only way we knew how to deal with it was to get together and get drunk every night.

Before Lenard was sent away to state prison, we decided to go down and see him at the L.A. County Jail. I didn't want to go because I didn't know if I would be able to deal with seeing him paralyzed and locked up, but in the end, I thought it would be good for him to see us. Maybe if he saw me and the others, we'd be able to give him some kind of hope.

On the day of the visit, Donti wasn't able to go, so it was just me, Rhonesia and Lenard's girlfriend. Just sitting in the waiting area, I knew jail was not the place where I ever wanted to be. This was my first time being in a place like this and I couldn't imagine myself, Lenard, or anyone I knew being locked up in a place this cold. And, I'm not talking about the temperature. Everything about the jail felt cold, from the stone-colored walls to the hard benches we sat on. And of course, it wasn't like the people who worked there were friendly.

Rhonesia and I were quiet as we waited. I knew she and Lenard's girlfriend were as nervous as I was. Finally, a guard led us down a long, smelly hallway. My heart was beating fast for so many reasons. I didn't know what Lenard was going to look like, and I didn't know what I was going to say to him.

After we'd walked a few feet, I could see Lenard, sitting in a wheel chair, behind a glass panel, holding a phone in his hand. It was hard to believe what I was seeing. He looked like he'd lost at least fifty pounds and his hair was so thin, it had to be falling out. Lenard hadn't even been there for a month. If he looked like this already, what would he look like after serving his twelve-year sentence?

My eyes immediately started to water, but I was able to hold back my tears enough so that Lenard wouldn't see them.

As I held the phone, I sat there for a few seconds without saying a word. "How are you doing?" I finally asked him.

"I'm fine," he said in an upbeat manner that surprised me.

Then I sat there, and just listened as he joked with his girlfriend and Rhonesia. I didn't have much to say because I was still so angry with him for putting himself in this situation.

Lenard had a smile on his face the whole time, but I knew that inside he was hurting. He had to be. Who would want to be in his situation, locked up and paralyzed? But he was acting all jovial so that we wouldn't feel sorry for him.

We didn't stay very long; when we stood up to leave, Lenard waved as if we would see each other again tomorrow.

Seeing Lenard really had an effect on me. It made me all the more determined to take care of my own future. The end of the summer was coming and I had to decide - did I want to stay at UCLA or did I want to leave? Could I withstand the way Coach Steve Lavin was treating me? Or was I ready to explore other options?

There was no doubt that I loved the campus, the city, the college life, the weather, the prestige, and the respect that all came with being at UCLA. But being on that campus wasn't going to last forever. Eventually college would come to an end and when it did, would I still be playing basketball or not? Would I be able to have the career in basketball that I wanted?

The answers to those questions would be determined by what happened in the next two years. That's all I had left in my eligibility.

After I asked myself all those questions, after I analyzed the entire situation, I made the only decision I could - I had to move on. I had to go to another university. I had goals bigger than UCLA and beyond UCLA. I would never reach them if I stayed there.

I called Coach Merino for his help and guidance once again, and he agreed with me.

"Start looking for a university that would be the right fit for you," he said.

NCAA rules allowed me to go to another Division one school, but if I did, this time I would have to redshirt and then I would only have one year left to play. I would lose a whole year. That didn't seem like the smartest move to me, and I did have another choice.

If I went to a university that was part of the National Association of Intercollegiate Athletics (NAIA) and not the NCAA, with *their* rules, I could play without redshirting, giving myself two full years to play.

Universities that are part of the NAIA are typically smaller schools and the level of basketball, although still good, is not at the level of the NCAA schools.

A few days after I spoke to Coach Merino, he called me back.

"Kevin, have you ever heard of Azusa Pacific University?"

When I told him that I hadn't, he went on to explain that it was a Christian university with a winning tradition at the NAIA level. The school had a long time coach, Bill Odell, who Coach Merino knew personally.

And the good thing was that it was still in Los Angeles - twenty-five miles from downtown and thirty-eight miles from UCLA.

So once again, I found myself visiting a school with the prospect of playing basketball. Coach Odell and one of the assistants, Coach Jim Hayford made me feel very comfortable when I arrived.

"Do you want a tour of the campus?" Coach Odell asked me.

I shook my head. I'd seen enough campuses. This time, I only wanted to see the gym, the locker room, and the weight room, and that's exactly what I told them.

But to my surprise, they showed me almost the entire university anyway, taking me into different buildings and different departments - none of which I was interested in.

It seemed to take forever to get to the weight room. It wasn't as big as the ones at Nevada or UCLA, but it was good enough. For some reason, the coaches were taking their time getting me to the gym and the locker room. It was as if they were reluctant to show me that part of the school and I began to get suspicious. We finally got to the point where there was nothing else to show me - it was time for me to see the gym.

When we walked in I couldn't believe what I was seeing. No wonder they kept me away for as long as they could. This had to be one of the smallest gyms I had ever seen. At the University of Nevada-Reno, I had played in the Lawlor Events Center which had a capacity of 12,000 and Pauley Pavilion at UCLA with a capacity of almost 13,000. This place, called the Cougar Dome, couldn't have had a capacity of more than 1,500.

In the locker room, surprise number two came. The basketball team didn't even have their own locker room. We had to share it with other teams, and the smell was funky and foul.

At both of my other schools, the basketball team had their own personal lockers and the room was laid out. It was a place where we could hang out, watch TV, and relax. This locker room was strictly for changing clothes, and maybe to take showers if you were brave enough.

Even with all of that, a few days later I made the decision to attend APU. It was all about basketball for me and I wanted to play. Clearly, it was going to be a big adjustment for me to adapt to the smaller facilities *and* attend a Christian university. I wasn't sure if I wanted to be walking around campus with a whole bunch of Holy people and having to worry about what I said. But even with those concerns, I felt like I had no choice. It was a done deal; I was a student at Azusa Pacific University!

***

When I arrived on campus, there was big buzz around the school about the guy who had just transferred from UCLA. I guess everyone already knew who I was.

It was cool, but I wasn't sure if I liked it because I couldn't decide if it was a good thing or not. There were many people who were excited about my arrival, but there were just as many who were not. Some of the other athletes from other sports were jealous of me for taking their shine away.

And all of that jealousy and envy hit the fan after I'd been at the school for only a few weeks. One particular night, my new teammate and roommate T.J. and I decided to go to a house party. The party was at one of the football player's homes, so most of the males there were on the football team.

Not too long after I arrived, a white girl came up to me and said, "KD, how you doing?"

At first, I didn't recognize her, but she reminded me that we'd met through a mutual friend at UCLA.

"Welcome to APU," she said.

"You're a student here?"

"Yeah," she told me. And then she added that she was here at the party with her boyfriend who was also a football player.

While we were talking, I knew some of the guys were watching us, but I didn't really think anything about it. We were just talking.

Finally, she told me that she would see me around, and when she stepped away, I asked another girl to dance. So there I was on the dance floor, minding my own business and partying when one of the football players jumped right in my face.

"Hey," he began. "I heard you trying to talk to my homeboy's girl." From his tone, I knew this dude was trying to start some trouble.

"I don't know what you talking about, but what you want to do?" I replied getting just as loud as he was.

This guy didn't know it, but he didn't want any trouble with me. I had a lot of anger built up inside. My life wasn't turning out the way I had planned. Here I was at this second tier school, with people I didn't know, and to top it all off, my girlfriend had just dumped me.

So I had come to this party to try to forget all of that and in the process, have some fun. Now, this guy wanted to test me.

"Let's go outside," he said, insinuating that he wanted to fight.

As he turned around, I grabbed his arm and swung him back, making him face me. Then I hit him as hard as I could.

He immediately dropped to the floor. I tried to get out of the house without having any other altercations, but when I moved toward the door, the boyfriend of the girl that I'd been talking to, came straight toward me with his fist balled up. Before he got the chance to raise his hand, I gave him what I'd just given his friend; I hit him as hard as I could.

Now I knew there was no way that I was going to get out of this house. That scared me, but I didn't panic. I made my way to the door, got outside, and before I could take a couple of steps, I was surrounded by at least two dozen people. Some were just trying to see what was going on, but most of them were football players who wanted to get to me.

As I was standing there in fear, I saw a bottle on the ground. I picked it up and started swinging. Anybody who got close was gonna get cut! There might have been some people there trying to help me, but I didn't know. All of these unfamiliar white faces surrounded me and I was going to get to whomever was trying to get to me.

Suddenly this one guy got a little bit too close for my comfort and I busted the bottle on his hand. Later on, the guy said that he'd been trying to help me. I don't believe that was true, but that's what he said.

Once I did that, I didn't have the bottle anymore as protection, and that was when the football player who started this whole thing jumped me. We fell to the ground and wrestled.

Finally, my roommate T.J. broke us up, got me up, and then shoved me into the car.

For the rest of the night, I was hot! I didn't even really want to be at this school and this was how I was treated after just getting here?

The next day, Coach Odell, called me into his office and he got straight to the point. "What happened last night, Kevin?" he asked.

Obviously, he'd heard about the incident, and so I told him the entire truth. I figured that it would be in my best interest to do that, even though I knew there would be repercussions. Maybe I shouldn't have hit those guys, but then again, I didn't start it, and I had felt threatened. So really in my mind, I hadn't done anything wrong. I was simply defending myself.

Coach Odell sat there listening, but for some reason, I felt like he didn't believe me. He never *said* that, but I was getting that vibe from his eyes.

"Well," he said when I finished, "the young lady said that you hit her and that's what started it all."

"What? She said that?" I couldn't believe it. Even though I knew she was trying to protect her boyfriend and his friends, I couldn't believe that she would just flat-out lie like that.

"What she's saying is not true," I told the coach. "And to prove it, I'll tell you my whole side again, right in front of them. And then, let her and her boyfriend, and his friends say their side of the story in front of me."

"That's not necessary," Coach Odell said.

What? He was refusing to let me do that? Didn't I have the right to face my accusers? How else would they find out who was telling the truth? Why wouldn't he want to get to the bottom of this? How was he going to just automatically believe their story and not mine? I was the one that he knew better than the football players. I was one of *his* players.

All of those thoughts ran through my mind and that's when I knew this wasn't going to turn out well for me.

The next day Coach Odell called me back into his office and told me the punishment that I would be given. It had come down from not only him, but from the university as well.

"You'll be suspended for two weeks. During the first week, you won't be allowed on the university grounds, and you won't be allowed to play any games. During the second week, you can come back on campus, but you still won't play."

Adding it up in my head, I was going to miss only three games during my suspension.

I guess that was a fair punishment. "What did the other guys get?" I asked.

With a straight face he said, "The football players are suspended for one-half of a football game."

For a second, I sat there stunned. Seriously! I asked the coach, "You mean to tell me that I'm missing three games, and I can't even be on campus for a week, and these guys are only missing a half of a football game?" Shock was all over my face and in my voice.

"Yes," he replied, simply.

At that moment I had never felt so discriminated against in my entire life. They didn't even bother to investigate the whole story. They took the word of the "white girl" and her friends. They assumed the white students were telling the truth.

When I told my dad what my punishment was and then what the other guys had been given, he was furious. He wanted to go to the school and demand explanations from everybody.

I had to calm my dad down before he turned that school out. "Don't even worry about it," I told him even though I was just as furious as he was, probably even more. But I couldn't let my father go to Azusa; nothing good would come out of that. This was my last opportunity to play college basketball; this was the bridge to my goal of playing professionally. So even though it wasn't fair and was a clear case of discrimination, I had to take it.

One thing my dad had told me a long time ago, and something that I'd never forgotten - You can throw a rock at an egg and it will break, or you can throw an egg at the rock and the egg will still break."

That was what I had in my mind at the time of the coach's decision. There was no way I was going to win this battle and there was no way I was going to let them break me. I only had one more year to play. I would just have to be strong during that year and keep my eye on the prize.

***

All of the adversity helped me to become so focused. I had an entire different mentality going into my senior year. I was not going to allow anything or anyone stop me from having my most successful year on the basketball court.

That year, it was all about basketball. I didn't go to any parties or any other social events. I pretty much closed myself off to the outside world. I had a key to the gym and every chance I got, I worked out. I worked out and practiced sometimes until three in the morning.

Even if a girl came to visit me, she became part of my workout. I would drag her to the gym and she'd rebound the ball while I ran drills. After that, we'd go hang out. If a girl didn't want to do that with me, then I didn't want to see her anymore.

It was all basketball, all the time and I didn't allow anyone or anything to distract me, not even my classes. I'm not proud of it today, but even when I was supposed to be in class, I would be in the gym.

It all paid off. When the year was over, I had earned almost every award that I could earn. I became an NAIA All-American and MVP of every pre-season tournament we played. I was the leading scorer and the MVP of the conference. I was also the leading contender for National Player of the Year, but since we didn't win the national title, I became the runner-up.

Along the way, I broke several school records including the most three pointers in a game and in a season. I was also in the top ten in every statistical category in my conference. No one had ever done that before.

Just like I planned, I had the best senior year I could possibly have. And just like I planned, that catapulted me straight to my career in basketball.

XII.

What Are You Going To Do

The thing always happens that you really believe in; and the belief in a thing makes it happen". - Frank Lloyd Wright

Riding on my collegiate senior year's success, I decided to leave school right after the season to pursue my basketball career. If I had to do it over again, I would have graduated first, but at the time basketball was my main concern. I was so into the sport, that I wasn't even able to concentrate on any schoolwork anymore anyway. So, it made sense that I left school.

I was invited to the NBA's Portsmouth Invitational Tournament in Portsmouth, Virginia. This invite-only camp was where all the top college players and potential NBA draft prospects played in front of NBA coaches and recruiters. The winner of the NAIA Player of the Year, and I were the only players in the country who were invited from a non-NCAA school. It was really a huge deal for me to be invited since I was coming from such a small university.

By this time, I had signed with an agent. When I called to tell him the exciting news of the Invitational and asked him to fly me there, he said, "Oh, you don't need to go. The chances that you'll make it are very low."

I immediately fired him, right then, and there. I figured if my agent didn't have faith in me, why did I need him?

Now with no agent and no money, I had to figure out how to get myself to Portsmouth, Virginia.

I didn't.

I couldn't get to Portsmouth and I missed out on that great opportunity. I'd really wanted to go, not only to play in front of the professionals, but I wanted the chance to measure my talents with the best players in the country. Hey, I thought I was good, but I wouldn't really know until I played against the best, right?

Missing the Invitational had me feeling really down, but I continued to work out hard with other players who had the same goals as I did. I was very fortunate to be in a circle that included legendary NBA basketball player Magic Johnson. Magic did something for us that, until I was older, I didn't realize how it impacted my life. It was something so simple, but very valuable to me.

Magic paid for all of us "struggling" professional basketball players' membership to a very upscale and very expensive sports club in Manhattan Beach. He also had the basketball gym reserved for us, giving us the opportunity to play with other NBA players.

So now I had a place to play quality basketball, a place to work out, and neither cost me a dime. I took full advantage of Magic's kindness. I went every day, played as hard as I could, and every improvement I made was because Magic believed in me and the other players.

Many years later, I played in the NBA Celebrity All-Star game. Magic was our coach and I got the opportunity to personally thank him for that.

After firing my first agent, I was in search of another one. I decided on an agency with three young guys who were new to the agent game, so they didn't have as many contacts as the others. But, I felt comfortable with them and I wanted to give them a chance. Two of them were Azusa Pacific alums so that influenced my decision, too.

A few months later, my new agents told me about an opportunity in Costa Rica. The team down there felt that I was the right fit for the job for two reasons: I had the skills they were looking for in a basketball player, and I could speak Spanish.

Speaking Spanish was a big plus; I'd be able to fit in with my teammates right away. But while playing ball in Costa Rica was a good opportunity, there was a huge drawback - it only paid $1,000 a month.

That was peanuts for a professional basketball player, but the job was during a time when most professional leagues were not even playing - the summer. So at least, I would be getting paid during the off-season. Not only that, but while playing, I would actually be training and preparing for the upcoming season. I would be able to get film of me playing as a professional to send to teams. So after weighing the options and the benefits, I took the job.

When I arrived in Costa Rica, it wasn't as much of a culture shock to me as it might have been for another player. Panama and Costa Rica border each other, so the countries had a lot of similarities. The people were real friendly and my teammates immediately embraced me as one of their own.

Playing there was not tough at all, and I immediately made a big impact. I quickly became the leader in scoring, putting up 40+ points in several games. On the social side, I got along well with my teammates and the fans loved me.

A month after I arrived, I received my first paycheck. I was speechless and full of joy. Not because of the amount of money - it was only $1,000 - but this check represented the fact that I'd reached one of my goals. This was the first goal that I had ever set for myself when I was a young kid - to make money playing basketball. Now, basketball was my career. With this check in my hand, I was officially a professional basketball player.

For about twenty minutes, I sat there, in my bedroom with the envelope in my hand, just staring at it. Tears fell from my eyes. This thousand dollars felt like a million dollars to me.

I'd always said, "Why not get paid for playing basketball? If no one paid me, I would still be doing it anyway, so I might as well get paid for it."

When the three month long season in Costa Rica was over, it wasn't easy to leave. I knew right then that place would always have a big part in my heart because it was the start of my career. Plus, I'd made friends that I hoped I'd keep for a lifetime.

After Costa Rica, the job offers came pouring in. I was able to get other basketball jobs in Australia, Taiwan, Turkey, and other countries. Whenever the sport was in season, I played basketball somewhere.

Playing in Australia was one of the highlights of my career. Not only is it such a beautiful country, but I loved the people. They were genuine, something that wasn't always easy to find. As professional players, we often meet people who are only nice to us and who want to be associated with us because we're basketball players, celebrities in their eyes.

But that was not the case in Australia. After being there for eight months, I realized that the people really cared for me, and their care and concern had nothing to do with my basketball playing abilities.

One time driving back from a friend's house in Melbourne to Geelong, the city where I played, somehow I got lost. It was only supposed to be a thirty-five minute ride, but an hour later I was still driving.

What complicated matters even more, in Australia, all the cars had the steering wheel on the right side *and* they drove on the opposite side of the street from what I was used to. So every time I got into the car that the team had given to me to drive while I was in Australia, I really had to concentrate, and not revert back to what I knew from driving in the U.S.

But being lost had me focused on trying to find my way rather than on concentrating on driving. I made a turn, swung into the wrong lane and crashed into a SUV head on. Before I even got out of the car, I knew my car was completely destroyed in the front.

For a while, I just sat there with a blank look on my face, inspecting my body for injuries. Miraculously, I didn't have a scratch on my body. Not one. It was almost impossible to believe, especially since the front of the car was so mangled, it looked like I should have been dead.

I jumped out of the car to check on the people in the SUV. From where I stood, I could see three of them: A man in the driver's seat, a woman in the front next to him, and a young girl - about three years old - in the back.

"Is the baby okay?" I asked, feeling frantic. That little girl was my first concern.

No one answered me.

"Is the baby okay?" I shouted over and over.

The man, who I assumed was the father finally replied. "Yes," he said sounding angry. "Everyone is fine."

Thank God, I thought to myself. Although the cars were destroyed, no one was hurt.

That was a blessing, but I was still so concerned. What was the team going to say? What would they do to me? I rushed to my cell phone and called Sue Wright, a lady who was very close to the team, and who had been there for me from the time I arrived in the country. She was like my Australian 'Mum', as they say in Australia. She cooked for me and helped me to get acclimated to the country. Anything that I needed, she was there to get for me. She had such a big heart; all she wanted to do was to make my stay in a foreign country a pleasant experience.

So of course, I called her first. Especially since I was so scared. I was sure that I was going to be fired, and then deported from the country - all for having an accident.

But Sue calmed me down and assured me that everything would be all right. She was right. Once I hung up from her, I called my coach and his only concern was about me.

"Are you all right, KD?"

I told him that I was and from there, he took over. Everyone understood that it was an accident and no one was mad at me at all. The next day, I was even given a replacement car while they fixed mine.

I had gone to Australia at a time when the best Australian basketball league, the first division, had just finished. The plan that my agents came up with was that I would go to Australia and play in the Second Division.

"Go down there and have a great season," one of my agents told me. "Then all the First Division teams will want you. You'll have all kinds of contracts coming at you."

I figured that I could do that. It was the Second Division, after all. But it turned out the Second Division wasn't easy. A lot of players from the First Division played because the two leagues were at different times of the year.

Still, I expected to play well since I'd been honing my skills and getting better every day. So, it was a shock to me that my first game was a disaster; I only scored ten points.

I was disgusted and after the game, I locked myself in my room. Seriously -I only came out of the room for practice. That was something that I'd been doing for a while. Whenever I had a bad game, I didn't want anyone to see me until I played in the next game and redeemed myself.

During my week of hibernation, I only let one friend come visit me; a woman I'd met when I first arrived. I was still depressed about my first performance and was trying to stay focused when she walked in, looked around and said, "I think I know what's wrong."

"What do you mean?"

"It's the way your furniture is arranged. Especially your bedroom. It's bad Feng Shui," she said, shaking her head.

I frowned. "Fong what?"

She went on to explain that Feng Shui is an ancient Chinese technique that brings harmony into your life with furniture alignment, colors, and other elements. Good Feng Shui can improve your health, career, relationship, and any facet of your life. Just like that, I was introduced to Feng Shui.

She started to move my furniture around and proceeded to give me a crash course on the art of Feng Shui. At the time, I didn't know what to think, but after that bad game I was willing to try anything. Just show me where I needed to push my bed and I was ready! We pushed and shoved my furniture all around, rearranging everything.

And then, I played my second game: I scored 25 points, had 11 rebounds, and 4 assists. From there, I never looked back.

It didn't matter how many players were from the First Division, I became a scoring and dunking machine. For me to have a couple of spectacular dunks in a game became a regular thing. I became the player to watch in the league.

Hey, maybe this Feng Shui stuff really works, I said to myself as I continued to grow into the player that I wanted to be. I wasn't sure if it worked or not, but you best believe that I left all the furniture where my girl told me to leave it.

And when the season ended, my game stats were great. I'd averaged 28 points, 9 rebounds, and 4 assists per game. I shot 50% from the field and 36% from the 3-point line. I'd scored 50 points in one game, and I was the leading scorer for the entire league. I was in the top ten in every category, just like I'd been in college. I was named the MVP, top scorer, and first team all-conference. No one had ever had this kind of success in the Australian league before.

I'd played up to my potential, just like I planned. And just like my agents planned, all the teams from the First Division wanted me on their squad.

I was very tempted to sign with one of the teams, but in the end, I decided against it. I truly loved Australia, my teammates, and the people of the country where I played. But I wanted more for my basketball career than Australia could give me. I was looking for more prestige and more money. So even though it was hard for me, I didn't return to Australia for a second season.

Over the next few seasons, my agents were able to get me jobs in several leagues around the world, but I never got that big paycheck - $100,000 or more - that I was looking for. I was always paid well enough to live while I played, but when I returned home, the money only lasted for few months and then I was broke again.

After every season overseas, I had to return to the U.S. and live with my dad. My dad had long ago turned my bedroom into an office, so whenever I went back, I had to sleep on the couch. Think about that - I'd lived and played around the world. People cheered me and respected me. Yet, after the last game was played, I was sleeping on the couch because I was never offered a contract in one of the premier leagues. It wasn't because of my ability; I think my agents just didn't have the contacts and connections. But I didn't want to leave them; they had worked hard for me, doing what they could with the people they knew. And I was loyal.

But then one day, my dad asked me something that would change my life: "What are you going to do?"

I was confused by the question, not exactly sure what he was asking me. "What do you mean?" I questioned him.

"What do you plan on doing with your career?"

"I'm going to play basketball, that's what I plan on doing."

But, I knew what my father was really asking, even though he didn't come right out and say the words. He realized I wasn't making the type of money that I should have been making and with his question, I was afraid that my father was telling me that he was giving up on my dream.

"You can't keep doing this," he said, pointing to the sofa. "You're not a kid anymore."

Part of the challenge was that every morning when my dad left for work, there I was, asleep on the couch. And when he returned from work, I would still be there; this time, lounging around watching TV.

What my father didn't realize was that in between 5:00 am when he left and when he returned in the early evening, I had a full day. I was up at 6:00 am running sprints, and doing long distance runs at Compton College with Deandre Austin, a good friend of mine. I followed my running with a shooting workout, then came home, ate lunch, and relaxed for a couple of hours before I was out again, either doing another workout or playing games at UCLA with NBA players and other pros.

By the time my father came home, I was done. But all he ever saw was me sleeping or watching TV. He never saw the hard work that I was putting in in-between.

"Okay, Dad. I'll be out of here by Monday." I said with a lot of anger and hurt inside me.

Now there were two problems with what I said. First, it was Friday, so that only gave me a weekend to move out. And, I didn't have any idea where I was going to go. But, I knew that I had to be out of there. I felt like he didn't believe in my dream any more. So I wanted to get as far from that apartment as possible.

I called Keith Hollimon, one of my agents, told him what was going on, and without hesitation, he said that I could stay with him and his family. At the time they had a three-year-old son named Kendal, but still they welcomed me with open arms.

I didn't feel totally comfortable moving in there. I was so independent, and didn't feel right imposing on them. But what else was I going to do?

So, I moved into the Hollimon's new home in Altadena, California. They set up a blowup mattress on the hardwood floor of the living room for me and, surprisingly, it was more comfortable than my dad's couch.

I kept up my same regiment, working out all day so that I would be in shape for whatever league I would play with when the season began. My mind was just on getting in shape, so I was surprised when one day my agent's wife,

Kathy told me that she wanted to introduce me to a good friend of hers.

"I really want you to meet Toi," she said, as she showed me pictures of her.

Picking up the photos, I couldn't stop staring at them. Toi was absolutely beautiful. "Sure, I'd love to meet her," I told Kathy. And that was the truth; I couldn't wait to meet her friend, though honestly, I was a little intimidated.

First of all, Toi was thirty-three and I was only twenty-four. And not only was she so much older than me, but I was at a point in my life when I had absolutely nothing. How could she possibly be interested in a twenty-four year old kid who was sleeping on someone's blow up mattress?

But she was so beautiful, I wanted to take the chance.

While I had my doubts about meeting Toi, little did I know at the time that she had doubts too. Later, I found out that when Kathy called Toi and told her that she wanted her to meet one of Keith's clients who was staying with them, Toi didn't want any part of it. Kathy had tried to set her up with guys in the past and it had never turned out well. But even with that, somehow Kathy was able to convince her to meet me anyway.

I was so anxious the night Toi was coming over for dinner. And when the time finally came and she walked into their home, it was like watching a slow-motion movie. I swear that I saw white doves flying above and her hair blowing in the wind, even though we were inside. She was beautiful when I saw her pictures, but in person, she looked one hundred times better.

After the introductions were made, I grabbed Keith and dragged him to the back of the room.

"Man, she looks good," I whispered excitedly. "She doesn't know this yet, but she's going to be my wife."

Keith laughed, but I was so serious. He just didn't know it.

The rest of that night was magical. Toi didn't come alone; she'd brought her nine-year-old daughter, Alexia with her and I fell in love with both of them that day. It was more than her beauty that attracted me. Toi was classy, yet down to earth. And Alexia was adorable and just as outgoing as her mother. Alexia was talented, too; she sang for us that night.

After that dinner, I saw Toi a couple of times, always at the Hollimon's home. But it was never on a romantic level. She was actually in a relationship and she'd just come to meet me as a favor to Kathy.

Knowing that, I respected Toi and her relationship and so I never approached her or let on that I was interested. But it wasn't just my respect for her that stopped me from making a move. Where I was in my life wasn't conducive to being in a relationship with a woman like her. If and when I approached Toi, I had to show her that I was a mature man who could handle being in a serious relationship.

But don't get me wrong; I was still interested. And I had a plan to win her over. I was going to take it slow, become really good friends with her first. And while I travelled and played around the world, I'd send her emails every now and then just to say hello. Then when I was ready, if she was by any chance single, I'd go all in and strike like a snake.

Toi was still on my mind when I took my next basketball job in Holland. I was in a very small town called Almelo near the border of Germany. I was the only foreigner on the team and all of my teammates were either in school or had daytime jobs, so beyond our games, there was no one for me to hang out with and nothing for me to do. The town was so boring that I had to either drive to Amsterdam, which was about an hour and a half away, or drive to Germany, which was about an hour.

But even though it was far, I made the drive anyway and on one of my trips to Germany I met a girl from Shreveport, Louisiana who was also playing basketball in Holland. Brandi was playing in a town not too far from me in the Netherlands and she was in Germany for the same reason I was - to have some fun.

We hit it off right away and started hanging out on a daily basis. It was a good thing that we were there for each another because I'm telling you, there was nothing else to do. So in between practices and games, Brandi and I would get together, hang out, watch movies - anything so that we wouldn't be bored.

The more we hung out together, the closer we became and eventually, we started dating. It was inevitable since we only had each other. After our seasons were over, we decided to really give our relationship a try.

"You should come back to Shreveport with me," Brandi said.

It didn't take a lot of convincing since I didn't have any place to live in Los Angeles nor did I have a whole lot of money. So, I returned to the U.S., to Louisiana where I was going to live with Brandi and her mom.

But surprisingly, being in Shreveport was almost like being in a foreign country. It was very different from what I was used to in Los Angeles. Louisiana was much more slow-paced, and it seemed like everybody knew each other. It was an old-fashioned kind of town that was nice enough, but not as modern as what I was used to.

My girlfriend had a lovely family, though. Her mother and her relatives who all lived nearby, embraced me as if I was one of their own. I loved the love I received from them, I loved how family oriented they were. But there was still one thing missing from my life. And it was major - basketball.

It was hard for me to find a place to play with other professional basketball players. I did contact the local junior college, and I worked out with players there so that I could stay in shape, but it didn't take long for me to start feeling a little depressed. The thing I loved the most, I couldn't do. I didn't have a place to play quality ball, and that meant that I wasn't improving. I wasn't improving because I was playing with players who didn't challenge me.

As much as I loved being with Brandi, as much as I loved her mother and her family, I made the decision to return to Los Angeles. It was hard leaving Brandi, and we made plans for her to come and visit me. We were going to find a way to stay together.

So after only three weeks in Shreveport (that's all I could last; not even a full month), I was back in Los Angeles. And back at home, I had everything that I wanted: great basketball competition, lots of leagues to play in, friends and family.

But there were a couple of things that hadn't changed - I still didn't have any money, and I didn't have a place to stay.

I didn't know what I was going to do, but at least, I had basketball. And at that point in my life, that's what was most important.

XIII.

I Dunked On Michael Jordan

"Dare to live the life you have dreamed for yourself. Go forward and make your dreams come true." -Ralph Waldo Emerson

I n the summer of 2001, I moved in with my old friend, Donti. He, his wife, and their young son lived in a small apartment and once again, I found myself in too familiar a situation. I was staying with great people, but I wasn't comfortable. I just didn't want to be in the way or interfere in their lives.

But like before, I didn't have any choice. So, I stayed with my friend, and I did my best to stay out of their way. Like always, I spent most of my days working out, playing basketball, and not returning to the apartment until night.

I didn't stay with Donti long; I never liked to impose on anyone for too long. So I left his house and was just moving around from friend to friend when one day, my agent introduced me to one of his friends, Mike Touhey. Mr. Touhey was the Mayor of West Covina, a city eighteen miles west of Los Angeles.

Mr. Touhey was a former basketball player who also attended Azusa Pacific University, and coincidently his family had connections to Panama. I think it was because of that connection, that he automatically took a liking to me. We often spent our time talking about Panama and his family's involvement in the Panamanian government.

When I met Mr. Touhey, I was one or two days away from living in my car. To this day, I don't have any idea how he found out about my situation since I'd never told him, and I'd never asked him for anything, but he offered me something I couldn't refuse. He offered me a room at a West Covina Holiday Inn for two weeks, free of charge.

Until he made me that offer, things were not looking good for me. Not that I'd lost hope; I always knew things would be okay, and Mr. Touhey made things okay for me - at least for the next two weeks. I will never forget Mr. Touhey for that kind gesture.

When I got to the hotel room, the first thing I did was take a trip to the grocery store. I only had enough money to buy a gallon of milk, a loaf of bread, a jar of peanut butter and a jar of jelly. That was fine because I would really be able to make that work. It would be my breakfast, lunch, snack, and dinner.

Of course things didn't have to be so dire for me. If I had shared more about my situation with friends, they would have helped me. But I never once told anyone how serious it was. I didn't want to be a burden, and I never wanted to borrow money. So I handled it on my own.

While I stayed at the hotel, I did what I always did - in between my "meals," I stayed busy with basketball. I worked out and played in all the summer pro leagues the Los Angeles area had to offer. Some days I played in two or three back-to-back games. To this day I don't know how I didn't pass out, doing all of that running up and down the court on a diet of peanut butter and jelly.

But that summer was a good one for me professionally. I played on teams that had many NBA players like Boston Celtic's Paul Pierce. There were many others and I kept thinking, "I'm playing with and against all these millionaires, and here I am, broke and starving."

Even under those circumstances, though, I stayed positive. I played well in every league, putting up some of my best stats to date. My goal, of course, was to still land a major basketball contract. I just knew it was a matter of time before that would happen.

The one thing about staying in that hotel for two weeks was that it took thinking about where I would live off the table. So for that time, my complete focus really was only on basketball. Like I said, I was never really worried; it always worked out somehow. And for two weeks, as long as I had peanut butter and jelly, I was good.

It turned out that staying at the Holiday Inn was only the beginning of my turn of fortune. One day, during my first week in the hotel, a scout for the Harlem Globetrotters approached me before I left the floor of one of my league games.

He introduced himself and said, "I like the way you play, Kevin; I've seen you play a couple of times."

"Thanks."

"Yeah, I think you have great skills, a lot of energy and the personality to be a Harlem Globetrotter. I'd like for you to come and try out for team."

At first, I didn't know what to think. "Wow, the Harlem Globetrotters?"

I had heard of the team and seen clips of them on TV, but I had never seen the Globetrotters play an entire game - live or on TV. But, I saw this as just another option for me, so I welcomed the opportunity.

The try-out was about a week long, and was right there in Los Angeles. Based on what I knew about the Globetrotters, I expected the try-outs to be about basketball tricks and lots of fun and games. But, boy was I was wrong. The try-outs were just like any other NBA workouts. I'm telling you, there was nothing easy about them. I had to go in there and play at my highest level possible.

There were about one hundred and fifty other players there, many of them either friends of mine, or guys I knew from the basketball circuit. But during that week, all of them were like enemies to me. They were standing between me and a basketball contract, and so I played hard. I treated every practice like a basketball championship game.

While others occasionally joked and played around during practice, I didn't. I was focused. I was determined. I was on a mission.

When the try-outs were over, I was satisfied. I didn't know what was going to happen, but I'd given it my best, like I always did, and that was all I could do.

About two nights before my two weeks at the hotel was up, I received that phone call - the Globetrotters were offering me a contract.

"The contract is for a year," the Globetrotter's representative said.

"Okay." That was fine with me. I had a contract! A six-figure contract!

"And there's just one other thing." The man paused. "You'd have to move to Phoenix right away. Will that be a problem?"

I laughed so hard inside - was this guy kidding me? I'd done my research, so I knew Phoenix, Arizona was where the headquarters for the Globetrotters was located. But would I move down there? Of course I would! There were only two days between the Holiday Inn and me being on the street.

"So, can you move to Phoenix right away?" the representative asked again.

I had grateful tears in my eyes when I said, "Yes! I can!"

It took me just one day to pack up all my stuff. When I left that hotel, I left my old school, Oldsmobile Cutlass

Supreme that was on its last leg parked right in the Holiday Inn's parking lot and I haven't seen it since!

I arrived in Phoenix ready to go, but to my surprise, I had to go through more try-outs. I had to compete against about seventy-five other players who came to town from cities all over the country. It was surprising because I thought they were already offering me a contract. But, no worries. I knew I could do it. I'd worked hard and made it that far. There was no way I was going to allow this opportunity to be taken away from me.

And it wasn't. I made the team!

At the time I signed with the Harlem Globetrotters, there weren't any games scheduled. But Mannie Jackson, the team owner, offered me an opportunity. He asked if I wanted to work in the Globetrotter's office for a few hours every day.

Hey, this was my chance to not only learn something about the team, but to also impress the boss by taking the opportunity.

So every morning I was up first thing, and in spite of the early morning wake ups, I enjoyed going into the office. I learned so much, especially how the Globetrotters operated from a management perspective.

My mornings were spent in the office, and in the afternoon, I worked out with Byron Smith, one of the coaches from Houston who had just moved to Phoenix like I had. Working out with Byron pushed me to my limits; he had me doing things that I never thought possible. He worked me out hard and he was certainly a formidable opponent. Byron was a good basketball player in his prime and he still played well, so we often got into heated one-on-one battles. He and I would workout and train for hours. In every work out, I wanted to beat him so badly. And sometimes, I did. But most of the time, he got the best of me. It was a good time in my life; I was happy being in Phoenix, thrilled with being a Globetrotter, and ecstatic about having my first contract.

But then, one day another opportunity came to me. It was so huge that it had the potential to change my life. I was home, just relaxing in my apartment, when my cell phone rang.

"May I speak to KD?"

"This is he," I replied, not recognizing the voice.

"I've been looking all over for you," the man said, sounding relieved. "My name is Nate Bellamey and I'm the owner of the Real Run Basketball league that you played in."

"Oh yeah, how you doing, Nate?" I said because I was being polite. But what I wanted to know was why was this guy calling me? And how had he even gotten my number?

"Let me tell you why I'm calling," he said. "I've been hired as a basketball consultant for an upcoming commercial." And then, he went on to tell me that I was being considered to be part of a Michael Jordan TV commercial. They were looking for someone who could dunk like Jordan used to back in the 90s, but who also had a similar body, skin tone, and height.

It seemed that the casting directors had spent months in New York, Chicago, Los Angeles, and other major cities; but no matter where they looked, they couldn't find what they wanted.

"There are lots of guys out there who can dunk," Nate said. "But then, none of them look like Mike. And the ones who look like Mike, can't dunk like him. Then, I remembered you playing in the league and I'm sure you can do it. I think you're the guy we've been searching for."

I sat there fascinated as Nate went on to tell me the vision they had for the commercial. It would feature the present-day thirty-nine year old Michael Jordan, who was currently playing for the Washington Wizards. He would be up against his younger self (the prime-time Chicago Bulls Michael) in a one-on-one basketball game.

"So, what do you think?"

I was flattered. I had a chance to be in a commercial with Michael Jordan? And play the young version of him?

All I could think was wow! Michael Jordan had always been my favorite basketball player of all time. How could I not see this as an amazing opportunity?

Nate was so anxious to get this moving that he told me he was going to fly to Phoenix the next day. "We can film you doing some of Michael Jordan's most memorable dunks and I can send it to the director."

We made arrangements to meet up at the gym, and the next day, the whole time I waited for Nate, I was nervous. I knew I could play basketball, I knew I could "Dunk like Mike," but I didn't know anything about being in a commercial.

When Nate arrived at the gym, he pulled out his camcorder. "All I need you to do are some Michael Jordan dunks and I'll film you playing."

So, I grabbed the basketball and did what I was used to doing. I would just dribble the ball, drive to the basket, and then, jump as high as I could and dunk. After every few dunks, I'd glance over at Nate. He held that camcorder steady, and I could see that big smile on his face.

The entire session only lasted about twenty minutes.

"I think I got what we need," he said. "I'll take this back and you'll be hearing from us."

A few days later, I got the call from Nate. "Well, I took it to Joe Pytka and you're the one he wants! We'll give you ten thousand dollars to do the commercial."

Ten thousand dollars? That was amazing. But it wasn't only the money that was incredible. I'd get to meet and work with Michael Jordan. And we were going to be directed by Joe Pytka. Joe Pytka was the biggest commercial director in the world. He had some of the most memorable spots including the "This is your brain on drugs," commercial.

I was thrilled to hear that Mr. Pytka was excited about me and he had told Nate to do everything he had to do to get me for the commercial.

I told Nate that I wanted to do it; I just had to get permission from the Globetrotters, of course. It was perfect timing too because there were no games on the schedule for at least a month.

The following morning, bright and early, I had a meeting with the Chief Operating Officer of the Globetrotters and explained the situation.

"That sounds like a good opportunity, KD," he said. "You can do the commercial as long as they put in writing that they will not be using the Harlem Globetrotter's name, your name, or showing your face in the commercial."

"I'm sure that won't be a problem," I said. "I'll make sure."

As soon as I got back to my apartment, I passed the information to Nate and within an hour he faxed over a letter with all the information that the Globetrotter's management requested.

I was on my way. The next day, I took the letter over to the C.O.O.; he reviewed it, and then said, "You're not going to be able to do this, KD."

"What?" I said, shocked by that.

"We're not giving your permission to do this."

Wow! I'd done everything that he'd asked me to do and now he was saying no? And he didn't even give me a reason. All he said was no - end of conversation.

I was pissed, but what could I do? I had no choice but to turn the commercial down because I couldn't risk losing a job that was paying me six figures for a commercial paying $10,000. Yes, that was a lot of money for three days of work with my idol, but the Harlem Globetrotters had spoken.

When I called Nate, I could hear in his voice that he was as disappointed as I was.

"I just can't do it," I told Nate. "I just signed this contract, and it's a lot of money. I wish I could, but I can't."

"I understand," he said.

I wished him luck with finding someone to do the commercial and he wished me luck with my career. I was really bummed about it, but then, a few days later, I got another call - from Nate.

"Look," he began, "Mr. Pytka really wants you and he's prepared to pay you whatever the Globetrotters are paying you."

"What?"

Nate repeated what he said. "Whatever they're paying you for the entire year, Mr. Pytka will match that."

"Wow!" was all I could say. "Okay, give me a couple of days to think about it."

"I'll give you two days, KD, but we have to make a decision."

"Okay," I said. "I'll get back to you."

I hung up that phone, and just couldn't believe this offer. Six-figures for three days worth of work? But I'd only been with the Globetrotters for a month. We hadn't even played a game yet. How could I leave now?

Not knowing what to do, I called everyone I knew who I thought could give me good advice. Most of my friends and family said the same thing.

"You've got to do the commercial!"

"The commercial is the smartest thing to do business wise."

"Six figures for three days? You've got to do the commercial."

I used the entire two days that I'd been given, but I made a decision. I decided to do the commercial.

A few days later, I flew to Chicago without saying anything to the Globetrotters. What was there for me to say? I knew what they were going to say, so I went to Chicago to start the first day of filming.

As I was changing in one of the United Center's locker rooms, I kept thinking, I can't believe I'm getting ready to meet and work with Michael Jordan.

I couldn't count the number of times I'd watched him play on TV and never once did I think I'd have the chance to meet him, let alone work with him. How often had I dreamed of wanting to "Be like Mike." And now, here I was...I was about to *be* Mike. "

As I walked out of the locker room, I felt all kinds of nerves going through my body. I was dressed to look like Mike in the old days. I wore a tight-fitting replica of his old Chicago Bulls jersey and my shorts were extra short, exactly the way the players wore them in the old days. I had on a pair of the first Air Jordan shoes, and a black and red sleeve on my calf.

When I got to the court, there was Michael Jordan waiting for me. Let me repeat that - Michael Jordan was waiting *for me*. I was so nervous, but I knew what to do. Reaching my hand toward his, I was just about to introduce myself when he said, "How you doing, KD?"

He knew my name?

"I'm fine, thank you. Nice to meet you, Mr. Jordan," I replied trying to hide my nerves. I hoped my voice wasn't shaky.

On the court, Jamal Crawford, an NBA player, was also there, dressed exactly like me. Later, I found out that they had booked him to do the commercial. But when they found me they decided not to use him. After that first day, I never saw Jamal again.

The producers gave me a little time to warm up. It took me about two minutes. I was so excited and so full of energy that I didn't need much time to get ready.

We filmed a couple of scripted scenes, but about eighty percent of the commercial was unscripted. It was just going to be me against Michael, playing one and one like two competitors on a playground.

So that's what we did. Just played. When we first started, I was still really nervous. It was hard to be my usual confident, fearless self when I was playing against the best basketball player ever.

And, I was scared, too. I didn't want to play him in a way where he would end up being mad at me. I didn't want to foul him; suppose he got hurt? Can you imagine? Michael Jordan gets hurt and it was my fault?

All of that was going through my head. But then, something happened. Something happened that changed me. He did something that I couldn't forgive and it snapped me right back to my usual confident and fearless self.

Michael Jordan dunked on me!

A basketball player dunking on you is the most embarrassing act that could happen on the basketball court. And no one dunks on me! I was the dunker and now there I was getting dunked on.

Now yeah, it was Michael Jordan. And some guys would accept that. But not me.

After his dunk, Michael walked off saying, "Y'all didn't think I could still dunk!"

He was smiling and when I looked around, the whole crew - the cameramen, director, make-up artists, everyone in the whole building was laughing - at my expense. The grin on Michael's face got wider, I knew that he was enjoying the moment.

Oh nooooo! There is no way I'm going to allow this to continue, I thought to myself. I got myself psyched up. I didn't care anymore that this was Michael Jordan. I was going to be Kevin Daley!

That was when it got real competitive. Three plays later, I had the ball and I was at the top of the key. Michael Jordan was right on me, playing hard defense. I faked left, took two hard dribbles to the right, and jumped as high as I could into the air.

At the same time Jordan jumped and stretched his arm out to try to block my shot, but he missed, and I dunked - real hard. The ball went through the net, then hit him hard on his face.

Yes! Inside, I cheered. I got him back for dunking on me. Now, I dunked on Michael Jordan. I was so proud.

Looking around, I expected to see the same people: the cameramen, the director, the make-up artists, and the whole crew laughing the way they had just a few plays earlier.

But nope - didn't happen. The entire United Center was dead silent.

I was full of confusion.

Michael was the first to speak up. "Hey young fellow," he said, "don't you forget this is only a commercial." He frowned, as he rubbed his face where the ball had struck him.

I didn't respond, but I was thinking, Hey, you didn't say that when you dunked on me.

That's when I knew this was a battle that I wasn't going to win.

But for the rest of the time, throughout the course of the three days, we had a really good time. In between takes, Michael and I talked and I was pleasantly surprised to see just how down to earth he was. He never once made me feel like he was "Michael Jordan" and I was beneath him. He made me feel like we were two old buddies, two equals just hanging out and having a good time.

That commercial ended up being a featured super bowl commercial that year and was said to be one of the greatest commercials of all time. Michael Jordan actually said it was one of his favorites.

After filming that commercial, I clearly was no longer with the Harlem Globetrotters. So, I went back to Arizona, packed my bags, moved back to California and made a few more commercials. Some of the commercials were with Michael Jordan, but most were without him. After that commercial, I even had a few movie roles offered to me. But I turned down all of it to go play basketball overseas.

Now don't get me wrong, I loved acting and would have loved to be an actor, but it always took a back seat to basketball. Even the commercials took a back seat. If it came down to me doing a commercial or leaving the country to play, the decision was always basketball.

Interestingly enough, just a few weeks after the commercial was filmed, I received a call from the Harlem Globetrotters. At first, I was excited - they wanted me back! But my excitement was short-lived.

The Harlem Globetrotter's management wanted me back on their team, but for considerably less money.

"What happened to the six digit contract that you offered me just a month ago?"

"We're not offering you that now," the Globetrotter's representative said.

I told him that I was the same player that I was a month ago. If I was worth that much then, today I'm worth the same. And so, I turned the Harlem Globetrotters down.

A few weeks later, I ended up going for a try-out in Beirut, Lebanon. I always enjoyed traveling to different countries and seeing different cultures. I formed opinions of the places I traveled to on my own, never relying on just the U.S. media, which could sometimes be negative.

But I have to say, I didn't know what to expect in Lebanon. When I got there in September, the weather was great, mostly in the high 80s, just like I liked it. And the beaches were spectacular with clean sand and clear blue water.

But what fascinated me most was the differences in the country. Parts of the country were filled with all the evidence of past wars: bombed out buildings, land filled with the ashes of burned down structures.

But at the same time, there were plenty of expensive cars everywhere: Ferraris, Porches, cars that I know cost upwards of $100,000 were very common.

I made the team after the try-outs, but once the season started, things were not going as well as I'd hoped. My coaches were forcing me to play a position that was not natural for me. During my entire career, I played the two and the three positions, which is the shooting guard and small forward. But my coaches wanted to turn me into a 1, a point guard. I was up for the challenge, but I was failing.

And then one night while I was resting in my apartment after a long day of practice, one of my Lebanese teammates called and told me to turn on the television.

"Something's going on in the U.S.," he said.

I turned on the T.V. expecting to have to search through the channels to find what he was talking about, but I didn't have to turn the channel at all. In fact, every channel was showing the same thing.

A tall building was burning, and at first, I didn't think anything of it - until I found out that it was one of the twin towers - the World Trade Center in New York City.

I stood there staring at the television in disbelief. I didn't understand the language, so I didn't know what the newscaster was saying. After the initial shock wore off, I turned to CNN in English. As I watched and listened to the details, another plane crashed into the other tower. I saw it with my own eyes and now, I was in complete shock.

It was hard for me to move around for the next few days without thinking about what was going on at home. At first, no one knew who was responsible for the attack on Americans. And then, it was revealed that it was Osama Bin Laden.

Even though he was not from Lebanon, I immediately thought I could be in danger being in Beirut. I wasn't American-born, and I wasn't even an American citizen yet, but people always assumed that I was American.

I never felt threatened at any particular moment. It was more like when I left my apartment, I felt like everyone was staring at me. I kept telling myself that I was just paranoid. Still, I wanted to leave. I was unhappy with my basketball playing and I was paranoid. Lebanon turned out to be a great place, but it was just my to go.

There was only one small detail stopping me. The entire world had grounded all planes.

For days, there were no flights or limited flights from every airport in the world. So, I was stuck in a foreign country with people that I didn't even know at all.

A few days later, I was able to catch a flight out of Lebanon to Greece - and once again, my travel was for basketball. There was a Swedish team in Greece playing a tournament, and they wanted to give me a try.

So, at least I was out of Lebanon. Greece it was!

XIV.

Kevin "Special K" Daley Is Born

"Nothing splendid has ever been achieved except by those who dared believe that something inside them was superior to circumstances." -Bruce Barton

B y the time 2004 rolled around, I was twenty-seven years old, and finally on my feet. I had my own apartment, and between basketball and the commercials I'd been doing, I had money in the bank. Residual income was coming in from all the commercials I'd been doing.

I was living a great bachelor's life. I had countless numbers of girls going in and out of my apartment. Friends came by and we'd play video games all day. I was free to do whatever I wanted, and had no one to answer to.

But even though it was a good life, at my core I felt like I was missing something. I had an empty feeling inside and I began to think it was all about companionship. Yeah, I had a lot of girls, but I didn't believe any of them were that special one and that's what I wanted and needed in my life - a special woman.

It had been more than a couple of years since I'd seen her, but no matter how many women I saw, I'd never been able to get Toi out of my head. And now that I was single and living well, I thought about her often.

I was living in Culver City; a city in Los Angeles County and I found Toi's number and called her. She was living and working twenty miles away in Pasadena, but once we connected again, we talked every day, even while she was at work. The more I talked to her, the more I liked her. And the more conversations we had, the more I wanted to see her.

She worked about a forty-five minute drive away from my home, and traffic in Los Angeles is no joke. But I didn't care. It got to the point where I'd get dressed up, make the drive all the way out to Pasadena, and take her out to lunch - every day. We'd spend about forty-five minutes together before I drove her back to work, gave her a hug, and then be on my way back home.

Even though we spent all that time together, I was so intimidated by her. She was so beautiful, very smart and very classy. And remember, she was older than me. With all of that, I was scared to make a move.

Well, I guess she got tired of waiting for me because one day, as I dropped her off from one of our lunch dates, I reached over to give her our usual hug. But as I leaned toward her she kissed me! Really! She gently planted a kiss right on my lips.

That kiss probably lasted only for a fraction of a second, but it put me in shock. My heart started beating faster, and I felt like it stayed that way on the whole drive back to Culver City. Even when I got home, I could still feel that kiss on my lips.

Up to that point, I hadn't been sure about Toi. I thought that she liked me, but I just wasn't sure *how* she liked me. Did she like me as a friend? Or could she see herself in a relationship with me?

Well after that kiss there was no doubt in my mind. Toi was beginning to see me and like me the way I liked her. She saw me as more than just a friend.

From that day forward, I was more comfortable and confident. Now, at the end of our dates, I was the one who gave her a kiss.

As Toi and I started to see more of each other, she and her daughter Alexia started coming to my basketball games. I loved seeing them there, and I played extra hard, doing my best to impress Toi. But she never cared about my performance on the court. I could have a bad game and she treated me as if I'd had a great game. As time went on, sometimes she would critique me. "Why did you miss those free throws?" she would ask.

I loved having her at my games and in my life.

That same summer I auditioned for the movie Coach Carter. I killed it at the audition and I was offered a major role in the movie. It was an exciting time, but then, my agent found me a job playing basketball in Turkey.

And so you know what happened, right? While I loved acting, I loved basketball ten times more. Acting was the hobby, basketball was the passion. So, I turned down the role and accepted the offer in Turkey.

The only thing about joining the Turkish team was that Toi and I were getting closer every day and I didn't really like the idea of living thousands of miles away from her. But I was determined not to lose her while I was living and working on a different continent. So while I was in Istanbul, I called and talked to Toi almost every day. It was costly, purchasing calling cards over and over, but I didn't care. I did it without even thinking about it.

Then, our relationship went to the next level when one night on one of our calls, Toi told me that she was moving out of her place. "But, I'm having such a hard time finding another apartment," she said.

"Why don't you move into my place?" I asked. I'd kept my apartment in Culver City and it seemed like the perfect solution to me. I guess it was the perfect solution for her, too, because she agreed. About a week later, she and Alexia moved in, got settled, and that sealed our relationship. I knew then that Toi and I were serious. We were committed to each other now that we were living together.

A few months later, I returned home, earlier than I expected. I'd encountered something in Turkey that had happened to me before. It was one of the downsides of playing basketball internationally - sometimes, you had to fight for your money!

That's what I had to deal with in Turkey. My team had no chance of winning the league, but we still had a chance to win a big cup tournament. We were one of only four teams left in the competition, and if we won the next game, we'd play in the championship.

But for several weeks, the team owed me and I kept demanding my money.

"We'll pay you later," that's what they kept telling me.

I didn't like that answer at all. The team expected me to perform. They expected me to come to the games on time, and play. If I didn't fulfill my responsibilities, they wouldn't have been happy.

Well, that was the same way I felt about them not paying me. So when the day of the big tournament game came and the team bus was outside of my hotel ready to take us all to the game, I waited in the lobby for my coach.

"Do you have my money?" I asked him.

He shook his head. "We'll have it later in the week."

Then, I shook my head. "I'm sorry, Coach, but I cannot get on that bus until you pay me my money," I said, making sure he saw just how serious I was by the expression on my face.

My experience had taught me that if a team really needed you to play and you put them in a tough situation, then they would find a way to pay you.

This was a big game and I knew the team would rather play with me than without me, so if I was going to get my money, this was going to be the time for me to demand it.

"So, do you have my money?" I asked him again.

The coach just looked at me and walked away. I stayed there in the lobby and another team representative came over to try to convince me to get on the bus. But just like I'd told my coach, I wasn't going anywhere until I got all my money.

Then he walked away, and after about thirty to forty minutes had passed, my coach returned with an envelope in his hand. "Here's your money."

I grabbed it and inside, I thought, Yeah, all of a sudden you have money to pay me. But I still wouldn't get on the bus. Not until I counted all of the money. And it was a good thing that I did because sure enough, the money was short.

"Coach, this is only half," I said. Half the money didn't make me happy at all.

"I know," the coach said. "We'll give you the rest when we get to the gym."

"If you have it, why can't you give it to me now?"

Something wasn't right. They were trying to trick me, I was smart enough to know that.

"Look, KD, we'll give the rest to you at the gym," the coach repeated.

Okay, if he wanted to play games, I was going to play along, too. So, I took the money they gave me and I told my coach that I was going upstairs to get my things for the game.

"Okay," he said. "But hurry. It's a long drive and we're late already."

I dashed upstairs, got to my room - and stayed there. I never went back down. No matter how many times they called my room, no matter how many times they banged on the door, I didn't respond.

They tried everything, but there was nothing that they could do - except bring me all of my money. Of course, the money never came, so I'd done the right thing. They weren't going to pay me at the gym, they probably weren't going to pay me at all. That was the last time the team saw me.

The next day I went to the airport to catch a flight back to the United States. Hey, I was unhappy that I didn't have all my money, but at least I had part of it, right? So, I was headed home - except there was this one major roadblock standing in my way.

I failed to notice that during the time I was in Turkey, my Panamanian passport had expired and the Turkish immigration officials would not let me fly to the United States. If I had been an American citizen I would have been able to travel back to the U.S. with an expired passport. But, I could not do so being of another nationality. I was a permanent resident of the United States with a green card.

With my expired passport, I had three choices. I could buy a ticket to Panama and fix my passport there. Or I could find a Panamanian consulate in Turkey. Or I could get permission from the United States government to fly to the U.S. with the expired passport.

Well, I didn't want to fly to Panama. That would be time consuming and an added expense. There was no Panamanian consulate in Turkey, so that option was out. And getting permission from the United States government would take too long. But against all odds, I found a lady who worked in Turkey out of her home for the Panamanian government.

"As long as you have a valid green card, you can fly back to the United States."

I was happy to hear that, and so I went back to the airport. But no matter what that lady had said, the airport officials were not going to let me go to the U.S. with that passport. I tried to show them proof that I could do that, but they wouldn't listen to me.

I argued with them, but not too much. I was in a foreign country and there were a bunch of guards with big guns surrounding me and the airport officials.

After a few days of being stuck there, I finally found a way to get home. I purchased a ticket to Panama, but I made sure that the connecting flight was through the U.S.; I found a ticket that flew through Miami. Once I got to Miami, I bought a ticket to Los Angeles and finally made it home.

I was glad to be home, but it was a different place for me now. I'd left the United States living the life of a bachelor, but came back being in a full-blown relationship. I went from living on my own as a single young man, to living with a woman and her teenage daughter.

It truly was a big adjustment, but I liked being with Toi and Alexia, and I felt that I was ready. Now, don't get me wrong; the adjustment wasn't always easy, but the three of us managed our way through and we lived well together.

I'd only been home for just a few months, when Toi came to me with some life-changing news.

"Babe, I think I'm pregnant."

"Pregnant? Are you sure?"

Yes, she was sure; she was pregnant. At that moment of hearing the news, I panicked. Now life wouldn't be about just me. I'd have to always provide for my child. I was making good money, but it wasn't steady. My basketball money was up and down as I'd just experienced in Turkey. And, I still hadn't landed that big contract after I left the Globetrotters.

I had found a way to supplement that income by doing commercials, but that residual money was unpredictable, too. Some months I made $10,000, but then there were months when I was only able to bring home $100. I never knew what I had earned until I went to the mailbox, opened the envelope, and saw the numbers on the check.

I always tried to keep money coming in by auditioning for more commercials. But getting a commercial gig was never guaranteed. I had to audition for every spot and yes, I was having great luck at my auditions, but that was because I never had any pressure. If I got the part, it was good, but if I didn't, I really didn't care.

But having a baby would change all of that. I would have added pressure because now I would need the money from the commercials. I would be anxious on my auditions - I would have to do well.

After thinking about what I'd gone through in Turkey, and my overall income, I needed a job where I knew how much money I was getting in every check. And I had to know that I would always get that check.

It was those thoughts that made me reach out to the Harlem Globetrotters. In the two years since I'd signed with the Globetrotters and then left, they'd contacted me a couple of times asking me to come back. But every time, they were talking about less money than what they offered me at first and I just wasn't going to take that.

But it was different now. I needed that kind of job and I was pretty sure that they still wanted me. So, I made the call, told them that I wanted to join the team and was thrilled to find out that I'd been right. The Globetrotters did want me, though they were still offering me less than my original contract. But this time, I accepted it not only because I wanted to be able to provide for my child, but I knew that the way I worked I was going to be great. Then, they'd have to pay me more.

I was ready now. Ready to take on this new chapter in my life and once I had the contract in place, I asked Toi to marry me. And I was a happy man when she said yes! (See, I told you she was smart!)

We got married on September 15, 2004 in a very small ceremony at the courthouse in Norwalk. That was good enough for the both of us. Then shortly after, we moved to Phoenix since that's where I had to be for the Globetrotters.

Two weeks after we arrived in Phoenix, I had to leave for a two-week training camp. And not only that, I would be hitting the road right after we completed the camp. I wouldn't even have a chance to come home. My first tour with the Harlem Globetrotters would start and that first tour was no joke. It would take me to Hawaii, Jamaica, Australia, and Hong Kong.

I hated leaving Toi so soon after we married, but she understood - this was work. I had a family that I had to provide for now. We would miss each other, but I had to do what I had to do.

Training camp for the Harlem Globetrotters was as intense as it was the first time around, but once it was over I got really excited.

Our first game was in Hong Kong and I had every emotion in the book when we arrived at that arena. I was nervous, anxious, excited, scared, and I didn't know what to expect. I knew that I was well prepared, but I was still hoping that I wouldn't make any mistakes.

As I sat in the small locker room an hour before the game, I looked around at the veteran players. They were all upbeat, in a good mood; not one of them seemed to be stressed at all.

So I began to wonder, if no one else around me was stressing, why was I? I needed to be relaxed the same way they were. I put on my headphones, tuned in to some reggae, and began getting into it, bobbing my head to the beat.

As the music played, I looked at my game uniform: my warm-ups, my shoes, the famous white and red striped shorts, and the jersey with the number 21. I stared at it for a long time, and I just sat there as so many thoughts went through my mind.

I cannot believe that this is for me, I kept saying to myself. Here I was getting ready to play a game with the most famous team in the entire world.

I let my thoughts go back to my days in Panama, when I practiced during lunch, when I would go out on the court and work out, even if I were the only one - like on New Year's Eve. I knew back then that all of that hard work and practice would pay off and bring me to a day like today. I didn't know how or when it would happen, I just knew that it would. I just knew that something great would come my way. I never lost faith, I always believed.

The music and the memories kept my nerves under control, though I could feel myself getting more excited as the game time came closer. We lined up to go out onto the court and even before we stepped in front of the crowd, I heard the cheers. The people were screaming, and stomping their feet, anxious to see us.

"And now the moment you all been waiting for," the announcer's voice boomed over the speakers, "put your hands together for the World Famous Harleeeeeeeeeeeeeem Glooooooobetrotterrrrrrrrrs."

The sound of Sweet Georgia Brown blasted through the arena as we jogged onto the court. Although my teammates were with me, I felt like everyone in the crowd was staring *at me*. That didn't make me nervous. That's what I wanted - I wanted everyone to look just at me.

I was proud of where I was in life, proud of where I'd come from, and proud of where I was going. I wanted to show the entire world what I could do.

The game was so much different than our practices. In practice, it was drill after drill, but now on the floor for the game, it all moved so fast. We went from one play to the next real fast. Whenever it was my turn, I did what I was supposed to do and I did it well. When I sat on the bench and watched my teammates, I was just like the fans in the arena. I laughed, I clapped, I cheered as if I'd paid for an admission ticket. That was funny to me - to think that the first time I saw an entire Harlem Globetrotter's game, I *was* a Globetrotter.

Game after game, I became better and better. And of course, I didn't have nerves before the games anymore. Being a Globetrotter came natural to me, but it wasn't until one of the veteran players gave me great advice that I really began to understand what it meant to be on this team.

Kerion "Sweet Pea" Shine told me, "Whenever you dunk or do anything, just let your personality out."

That's all I had to do? Let my personality out? I began to understand. This was entertainment, so that's what I did - entertained.

After each dunk I scored, I celebrated in a different way. Sometimes, I ran down the court with my arms spread out wide like I was an airplane. At other times, I would act like I was an electric-guitar playing rock star. I came up with so many varieties, so many "personalities." I wanted to entertain the fans and so before each game, I spent about an hour thinking of a new celebration. And the fans loved it!

But the fans weren't the only ones appreciating my efforts. A few games into my first tour, at a game in Australia, the team's owner, Mannie Jackson walked into the locker room at halftime.

"Hey, everyone," he shouted, getting our attention. When we were all quiet, he continued. "You see this guy here?" He pointed at me. "He's doing some special things out there on that court. He's a special person and player. So as of today, his name is Special K!"

The guys laughed and cheered and Kevin "Special K" Daley was born right there in Australia!

As my first year went by, I started enjoying playing for the Globetrotters and everything that went with it more and more. People all over the world respected and appreciated us. Everywhere we went, every continent, every country loved us.

All of that just made me work harder on my craft and it made a difference because in less than a year I became the showman and captain of the team.

Now, the showman is the main person on the team. He's the face and voice of the Harlem Globetrotters. This was a special honor to me because of the showmen in the past: Meadowlark Lemon, Geese Ausby, and Twiggy Sanders. All of these men are Harlem Globetrotter legends.

But one thing about being out there with the fans -I found out that many of them knew more than I did about the Globetrotters. The fans knew their history and at times, it was embarrassing for me to run into someone who knew more about the Harlem Globetrotters than I did.

So as the showman of the team, I wanted to fix that. During my time off, I made it my business to gather anything that I could find about the Globetrotters. I went to the Globetrotters' office and raided the video room of all the videos the team had going back to the 1950s. Then, I purchased a VHS to DVD recorder from Best Buy and transferred all the videocassettes into the DVD format. After that, I was able to travel with DVDs everywhere I went.

Beyond the tapes of the team, I watched and studied all kinds of comedians. I particularly watched those who were great with physical comedy. Comedians like Lucille Ball, Mr. Bean, and Charlie Chaplin. I spent countless hours looking at their work and studying them.

I would watch an entire movie on mute to see which comedians made me laugh without me hearing a word. To me, physical comedy was one of the most important tools we had as Globetrotters because we traveled to so many countries where people didn't understand our language, but we still had to entertain them.

Because of what I learned, I began to really concentrate on my physical comedy. Everyone world wide could understand that.

I always knew I could make anyone laugh with words, but working on my physical comedy made me a much better entertainer. I already had the edge over all other showman because I could do 100% of the show in Spanish. No one in the 88-year history of the Harlem Globetrotters had ever done the entire show in another language until I came along. Now, all the Latin American countries could fully understand the show like never before.

I was able to help the Harlem Globetrotters go to another level.

XV.

Here Comes The Head

"A baby fills a place in your heart that you never knew was empty"-unknown

O f course, playing for the Globetrotters wasn't the only thing going on in my life. I was newly married with a baby on the way.

It was hard being away from Toi, especially since she was pregnant. After I left for training camp and the first part of my tour with the Globetrotters, I didn't return home for about a month and a half. And then, I was only home for about two weeks before I had to hit the road again. The next tour was the big one. I was away from Toi for four months and we weren't even able to spend our first holiday together.

I'm sure you can imagine how hard that kind of schedule and that kind of separation is for any married couple, especially newlyweds. That first year of our marriage, I really only spent a few weeks with Toi before we became parents together.

I returned home from that first big tour with the Globetrotters on April 15th and about a week later, I went with Toi to her regular doctor's appointment. She was getting close to her due date and I was more than just a little anxious as I waited for the doctor to see us.

My anxiety level increased even more when, after the doctor examined Toi, he told us to come in on Tuesday, the 26th.

"I'm going to induce labor," the doctor said.

The doctor's words scared me. Not that I thought anything was wrong with the baby. We had a good doctor and I knew he would take care of Toi and our baby. But I was really afraid now...I was about to be a father! Would I know what to do? Would I be able to handle it? I really wanted to be a good father, but I didn't know whether or not I would be.

Over the next few days, that fear just settled inside of me, building and building until the day we left for the hospital.

On that Monday morning, when we woke up, we were already prepared to go; Toi had had her bags packed for days, and she was ready for this. Much more ready than I seemed to be.

It all went rather smoothly at the hospital since they were expecting us. We were checked in and Toi and I were taken to her room.

I guess it's really very different when you have an appointment to give birth rather than giving birth naturally. We didn't have to wait long for our doctor to come in and begin the process.

It was a blessing for me to be in there with Toi. I sat by her side, holding her hand while the doctor induced labor. It seemed like very little time passed (at least to me, probably not to Toi) before the doctor was saying, "Here comes the head." And then, he added, "Mr. Daley, would you like to see this?"

What was so amazing was that I *did* want to see it. In the past, if I'd seen anything like that on television or in the movies, I would turn my head, not wanting any part of it.

But with my child, it was a wonderful, beautiful thing and I wanted to witness every moment. I watched the entire time as our child made her journey through the birth canal, seeing first her head, then her shoulders before the rest of her body eased to life.

When the doctor announced, "It's a girl," I was filled with so much joy.

"Would you like to do the honors?" the doctor asked me gesturing toward the umbilical cord.

It really was an honor for me. But once the nurse put my daughter in my arms...that moment was indescribable. To look down at her and know that I had created this life, and that I had brought her to this earth was overwhelming. I checked out everything, her hands, her fingers, her toes. I studied her face, wondering what she would look like and who she would look like. I looked for the parts of her that would be me, and how she would look like Toi.

I held her as if I was holding a piece of fine china, as if she would break at any moment. I had never felt so much love in my life.

When we went home, I hardly wanted to do anything except look at our daughter, whom we named Kaydee Veronica Daley. Veronica was my mother's middle name and now her name would live on with my baby.

I just wanted to look at her, and hold her and love her. And that's all I seemed to do. But then, the day came when I had to leave. I had to go back out on tour just two weeks after Kaydee was born. I really hated leaving her. Of course, I knew she would be in wonderful hands with Toi, but I hated leaving Kaydee because I was going to miss holding her, and kissing her, and being right there, being her dad.

But, I had to go to work. Kaydee was the reason why I had joined the Globetrotters...I had to take care of her and I wanted to do it well.

Just because I was away, though, didn't mean that I didn't want to be a part of Kaydee's life. Every day I called Toi and I would have her put the phone to Kaydee's ear so that I could speak to her. That was a promise I made myself. No matter where I was in the world, I had to communicate with Kaydee. I was going to make sure that I was never a stranger to my daughter.

That was my biggest fear - that I would be away for so long that one day, I'd come home and my daughter would say, "Who's this?" I was going to make sure that never happened.

But while I worked on building a great relationship with my daughter even while I was away, I fell into some bad traps my first year as a Globetrotter that affected my marriage.

It's not something that I'm proud of, but there were lots of women who were available while we were on the road. No matter what city, no matter what country, they were always there. And there were times, when I became involved with some of those women.

To me, I never thought that I was risking my marriage - I loved my wife. But being far away from her, often left me feeling lonely. That's not an excuse, it's just a fact.

But that's a fact that put my relationship with Toi in jeopardy. In fact, when she found out that I'd been unfaithful, she was so hurt that she wanted a divorce.

I was devastated. I hated that I'd hurt my wife, but I also didn't want to lose her because of my bad judgement. So, I fought hard to keep us together. Even though at first, she didn't want to talk about anything except for a divorce, I convinced her that I loved her and that all we needed was counseling.

Little did I know that I was right - I did need counseling. During that time that Toi and I spent with a counselor was so eye-opening to me. I discovered that some of the relationships I sought on the road may have been explained as me simply being lonely. The doctor was able to trace those feelings all the way back to my childhood - and the lack of a relationship I had with my mother since she passed when I was only three. From the moment she died, I craved that love of a mother, of a woman, really. And so, as I got older, I searched for that love, substituting love with women for the love that I missed with my mother.

Understanding that about myself made me promise Toi that I would work on that, that I would change, and that I would be faithful. It was a fight, but I did win her back. It was a fight, but I finally earned her trust once again. And with time and counseling, we were able to move on.

I was so grateful to my wife for believing in me and for giving me another chance. I was looking forward to a long and happy marriage with Toi. I wanted her to really be a part of my family - and that meant, she had to meet those who were most important to me. Beyond my brothers and my dad, she had to meet my grandmother.

My grandmother had moved from Panama to Killeen, Texas, a military town one hundred and fifty miles from Dallas. She was living with my aunt Norma.

I was excited about my grandmother living in Texas because that meant that she could come and see me play with the Globetrotters.

My grandmother had never seen me play basketball, not in school nor as a professional. But she was able to see me play as a Globetrotter, twice!

After the first time she came to the game, I asked her, "Grandma, did you see me play?"

"No I didn't," she said. Her eyesight wasn't as good as it used to be. Then she added, "But I heard your big mouth the whole game!"

Together, we laughed. She was right; she may not have been able to see me, but she could hear me since I played the entire game with a microphone.

I was so thrilled that my grandmother had finally been able to see me doing what I loved. And now that she was in the States, I couldn't wait for her to meet my wife and daughters.

As soon as my tour ended, my plan was to pack up Toi and the girls and drive to Killeen. I only had a few weeks left on the tour, so Toi was getting things ready at home.

But before the tour ended, before I could get in the car, just a week after I had that conversation with my grandmother...she passed away.

I was devastated. Not only because I was going to miss the beautiful, caring and loving woman who had poured so much into my life, but my family would never have a chance to meet her. They would never get to know the angel who took care of other people's kids as her own. They'd never meet the woman who'd feed anyone who came to the house, even if it meant that we all had to eat less.

My grandmother's passing was not easy for me. And it really showed at her funeral when I just couldn't stop my tears from flowing. It was probably the most difficult day of my life.

But I was happy about one thing. I was happy that Maude Daley was my grandmother. And that I was fortunate to have her in my life for as long as I did.

XVI.

I Won

"The successful man is the average man focused"- unknown

B y my fifth year with the Harlem Globetrotters, I had already traveled all over the United States, and to more than fifty countries. It was a very busy life with lots of time spent on planes, and tour buses. Each year, we traveled seven to eight months out of the year, so can you imagine how many nights I spent in hotel rooms?

One of those nights when I was just laying around, I began to wonder how I could maximize and really use my time while I was on the road. No longer was I into the nightlife the way I used to be, so often I found myself just hanging out in my room. So, I thought and thought and that's when it hit me. I could go back to school to finish my degree in Sociology.

When I left school back in 2000 to pursue my basketball career, I promised myself, and I promised my dad that I would finish what I had started. Although it was a good move to leave school then for basketball, (obviously it was good since I was able to build a career,) I decided that now was the right time to go back.

So I began my quest to find the right school. I researched the many universities that offered on-line bachelor degrees and that would accept my credits. Ashford University, a school in Clinton, Iowa seemed to be the best alternative for my situation. Each class would be accelerated, would earn me three credits, and would take five weeks to finish. I was twenty-one credits short of my degree, so it would take me about a year and a half to graduate.

I decided that was the school for me, so I enrolled. I knew this journey was not going to be easy, especially with the grueling schedule I had. But I also saw it as a challenge and I was up for it.

Many of my teammates laughed when they heard that I was going back to school. They didn't think I could do it.

"You'll be too distracted," they said. And they continued to voice all kinds of doubts.

But what they didn't know about me was that when someone doubted me, it motivated me to prove them wrong. I was happy to hear from those who thought I wouldn't be able to do it. Their doubts and their laughs helped me tremendously.

Just weeks later, I began my classes. Right away, I could tell that this wasn't going to be easy at all. I found myself studying in the locker room while music blared around me. And on the long bus rides when I was already exhausted. Any chance I had, I studied. Some nights we wouldn't get in to the hotel till well after midnight. But I didn't have time to rest. I had to do homework.

It was tough. I was tired and many times, I found myself getting discouraged. But whenever those moments came over me, I pictured the faces of those who doubted me. Those faces were my driving force.

I was completely focused on achieving my goal. No matter where I was, I got it in. There was the time when we were in Argentina, in one of the smallest locker rooms I'd ever seen. It was already hot and the way we were all stuffed in there made it worse. The music was blasting, my teammates were laughing, and I could hardly breathe.

But, I had a big research paper due the next day. And so with all that chaos around me, I sat with my laptop open, typing my paper. I had to look past the conditions and just get it done.

One of my teammates finally noticed me. "Hey, Special K, how are you able to work like this?"

I looked up, and with a straight face I told him, "I didn't even know you guys were in here!"

They laughed, but that's how focused I was. Nothing was going to get between my goal to earn my Bachelor's degree and finally graduate.

And that focus, that commitment paid off. I did graduate. I graduated with a 3.6 GPA, on the Dean's List and I graduated with distinction.

That's what focus will do for you! Just like every-thing else in my life that I set my mind to, I won.

XVII.

Represent From Panama

"Don't let success go to your head—and if you fail, don't let failure go there either." - Jane Seabrook and Ashleigh Brilliant

While traveling worldwide and playing for the Globetrotters, I always dreamed of the day I could have a Globetrotter game in my own country of Panama. I'd been playing with the Globetrotters for six years when that finally happened.

When the Globetrotters first told me that they had booked a game in Panama I was extremely excited. I couldn't believe that what I'd been dreaming about was finally going to happen.

I was a proud Panamanian, and I took representing my country very seriously. When I was introduced at every Globetrotter game, I made sure that before the announcer even said my name, he said, "From Panama City, Panama...."

I wanted everyone in the building to know where I was from. Even my theme song started with "Represent from Panama."

All of us Panamanians were proud. No matter what city or country I was in, if there was one person in the entire arena who was from Panama, they would find me after the game and tell me how proud they were to have a Panamanian as the leader of the most famous team in the world.

Their words always meant so much to me. I may have left Panama when I was twelve, but I never left the love for my country and the love for my people. So like I said, it was thrilling to be returning to the place I still called home.

A few days before the actual game, I was sent to Panama to promote the upcoming game. It was exciting times for my friends and family who were still living there. For the first time, they would see me play with the Globetrotters. They'd seen me play a few times when I played with the Panamanian National team starting back when I was in college. But they'd never seen me play with the Globetrotters.

When I landed in Panama, the airport was packed with media, friends, and fans. Cameras flashed all around me, blinding me as I walked into the terminal.

I headed straight for my friends, many of them my old neighbors from Pedregalito. I hugged as many of them as I could, thanking them for coming. Before I could do anything, I was hauled away by my friends who wanted me to go with them to Pedregalito.

"We have a surprise for you!"

A surprise? I had no idea what they were up to, but I was happy to be there with them and happy to find out.

We rode through the familiar streets and as I looked at the houses, it didn't even feel like I'd been away for so long. We drove past the home where I grew up, but we didn't stop there. My friends took me straight to the end of the block, to the court where I made my first basket ever.

To my surprise, the court was packed. Almost everyone from the neighborhood was there waiting for me. They cheered when I got out of the car, and I was overwhelmed. Seeing all of those people there just for me was too much. I never knew that so many people cared.

Music was blaring, there were hotdogs, hamburgers, and steaks on the grill, kids were running around, shouting and playing. It was an all-out celebration.

And the celebration was for me. My friends and neighbors were celebrating my accomplishments and I was so appreciative. I had never played basketball for just myself. I played to represent my family, my friends, my country, *and* myself. I had never told anyone that. I had never voiced it at all. But I was happy that my friends, neighbors, and my entire country noticed that I always tried to represent them, and represent them well.

For the rest of the afternoon, I took pictures with them and hugged just about everyone who was there. And everyone there was so proud of me. That's how we are. Us Panamanians are a very proud people. When one of us accomplishes something positive, everyone feels the joy.

Right as the evening was coming to an end, one of the neighbors led me to the far end of the court beneath one of the baskets.

"Look at this, Kevin," he said.

I couldn't believe it. Right there on the concrete was my name, *Kevin "Special K" Daley,* painted on the ground right where my dream began. What a thrill! Talk about being proud - this was a very proud moment for me.

As I was leaving, I found the lady who'd bought our old house from my dad.

"Would you mind if I went to the house with you and took a look around?"

"I wouldn't mind at all," she said happily and she took me right over there.

When we got to the front of the house, I stood, staring at it for a moment, a little hesitant at first. I couldn't believe that so much time had passed; it had been more than twenty years since I walked into that house. I'd been back to Panama, and had even walked past my house, but I hadn't been inside since the day I left for the United States.

There were so many memories, good and bad, memories that had impacted my life.

I took a few steps toward the front door. The outside didn't look the same; the new owners had made a few changes to update the look. But when I walked inside, I was immediately taken back to when I was twelve years old. It felt like a movie, like I was standing in a scene and seeing myself in the past.

As I walked through the house, every step brought back something different that I remembered.

I talked to myself: "Over here is where my dad had his sacred sound system that he didn't let anyone touch."

"Over here is where I used to eat and throw my vegetables behind the furniture so I wouldn't have to eat them."

"Over here is where I first learned to wash dishes."

Memories just kept rushing to my mind.

I saw a table right where our table was that held our red rotary phone. The new owner's phone was in the same exact place and just staring at it made my old phone number come to me just like that. I couldn't believe it because I could hardly remember my last cell phone number.

But at that moment, I remembered the number and I told the woman.

"That's funny," she said, after I told her the number. "That's my number. We kept your old number."

I had only spent a few minutes in her house, but I thanked the lady profusely. I hugged her to show her my appreciation and she gave me a strong hug back.

"Thank you for taking such good care of our house," I said. "This place meant so much to me and my family."

After that wonderful night in the neighborhood, the next day, I visited my old school, Instituto Episcopal San

Cristobal. And just like the day before, there was a crowd waiting when I arrived.

The entire student body was outside. Let me repeat that, the entire student body was outside *waiting for me*. And this was a large school that went from kindergarten to the 12th grade. I'd only attended until the 6th grade, but the school held a special place in my heart. Not only had I built life-long friendships, but this was the school where I'd joined my first basketball team. This was where my first coach taught me basketball fundamentals. This was where I used to get in trouble for playing basketball when I was supposed to be in class or studying.

Of course, I didn't know any of the students, but I was surprised to find out how many of the teachers were still there. The principal had been a teacher when I attended, and she had been a friend of my mother's.

She was the first one to pull me into her arms. "I'm so glad to see you," she said, giving me a huge hug. "You know I was so devastated when we lost your mother, and I think about you and your brothers all the time. But I'm so proud of all of you." Then, she took my hand and led me into the school. "You have to see the new gymnasium."

I was anxious to see the remodeled gym. About a year before, the school had contacted me for a donation as they were doing the remodeling. They'd asked people to donate enough to basically buy one brick.

"And in return for your donation, your name will be imprinted into the brick," the letter said.

My brothers and I all donated, so I wanted to see the bricks with our names.

When I walked into the gymnasium, there were more students waiting for me. The band was in there, pumping up the crowd, and it reminded me of my brother, Sergio, playing the saxophone in the band. I was amazed to see that the same band teacher was still there.

New memories flooded back to my mind. It felt like it was only yesterday when I was playing ball, running up and down this court. And I felt such a sense of pride when I saw the brick with my name on it.

While the band played, the folklore dance group performed a couple of special dances for me. As they danced, I reminisced. I used to dance with the folklore group.

After the dances, the principal said, "Kevin, there's someone here to see you."

I turned and there was Professor Villanueva, my first basketball coach. I had expected to see him, but seeing him was even better than I imagined. There was such pride in his eyes and when he hugged me tightly, I knew for sure that he was proud of me.

He asked me how things were going, how was it to play with the Globetrotters, how was it to travel all around the world. I could've stood there all day and chatted with him.

But then, I grabbed the microphone and turned to the crowd. I had my own surprise and it was for the man who really started me on this basketball journey.

"Years ago this man right here," I began with my arm around Professor Villanueva, "gave me my first basketball uniform ever. Today, I'm very proud to give *him* one of *my* jerseys." Right there, I handed him a Harlem Globetrotter jersey with the number 21.

As he grabbed it, tears dripped from his eyes. He slipped the jersey over his head and wore it proudly.

See for me, this journey that I had taken was always about making other people proud. It had been that way my whole life. I don't know why I was that way. Maybe it was because my mom wasn't there to tell me that she was proud of me, and I had to find that pride from other people. Well, I found what I'd been searching for, and this trip proved it.

But the pride didn't end there. Even the President of Panama was proud and he told me that himself. I was invited to spend some time with President Ricardo Martinelli, and as he shook me hand, he said, "Thank you, Kevin, thank you for representing Panama in such a positive way."

Then, we posed for pictures and after a few shots, President Martinelli said, "Kevin, why don't you sit here."

I was shocked, at first. He was offering me his presidential chair. What an honor. But I didn't realize how much of an honor it actually was until the picture appeared on the front page of the newspaper the next day.

"Do you know how big a deal that is, Kevin?" everyone asked me.

Apparently only presidents ever sat in that chair. The emotions that went through me when I learned that - I was filled with such joy.

After countless radio, newspaper, and television interviews, and visits all over Panama to see my family and old friends, game day finally arrived. I couldn't wait to show my skills, to show my country what I could do.

The bus ride on the way to the Robert Duran arena was like riding in a limo to the prom. I was filled with all kinds of emotions: excitement, happiness, anxiety...it was almost too much.

As I sat on that bus with my headphones covering my ears, my thoughts went to my mother. I so wished that she could have been with me to experience this day. No matter how old I got, my desire to have my mother stayed with me.

I had to push those feelings away, though. My mother would never have the chance to see any of this, so I had to focus on other, more positive things.

Even though we arrived at the arena several hours before the game was to begin, people were already gathered outside. As I walked toward the entrance, the crowd cheered, greeting us and many shouted my name.

In the locker room while getting dressed, I didn't do my normal routine. At every other game, I listened to music, danced around, joked with my teammates. But there was nothing normal about this game.

I was getting ready to entertain more than ten thousand people. Ten thousand who came to see *me* play. Now of course, I'd played in front of large crowds before, crowds that were even bigger than this. But this time, everyone was here for me. Just me. Not the team. Just me!

When it was finally time for us to run onto the court, we lined up. I was not nervous at all. Not until the announcer's voice screamed through the speakers, "And from Panama City, Panama...."

He couldn't get my name out. The crowd went crazy, cheering and screaming. The atmosphere was absolutely electric.   We started off with our Magic Circle, which is where we did our basketball tricks and I was trying my best to concentrate on not making a mistake. But to be honest, my entire body was shaking.

My eyes filled with tears of pride, as I did all my basketball tricks in our Magic Circle with "Sweet Georgia Brown" playing through the speakers. I had to fight to keep my emotions under control because I had fans, friends, and family in the crowd. This was not the time to mess up.

And I didn't. I was flawless! After the Magic Circle, I finally took a deep breath.

We finished with the tricks and went into our warm up. That was when I would shoot my famous half court hook shot. The shot that had put me in the Guinness Book of World Records. The shot that was 46'6" feet long.

I took this shot at every game, but I didn't always make it. It was a high percentage shot for me, though - I made it more than I missed it. But sometimes, it would take me a few attempts.

On this day, I walked up to my mark, full of confidence and in my mind, I said, Let me make this shot so the people can see that I really can do this.

I stared at the basket, smiled at the crowd, and then turned back to the basket again. I finally released the ball and as it was in the air, I knew it was a nice shot. It moved in slow motion, and as the ball got closer to the basket, I was sure it was good.

Finally, it dropped. Swoosh!!!! Nothing but net.

That was just another reason for the crowd to go crazy. Everyone was amazed and the game hadn't even started.

From the time we began, the crowd cheered. And we thrilled them. It was a great game; we'd given the fans something spectacular.

After the game, I stayed signing autographs and taking pictures longer than usual. But I didn't mind. This was Panama and I loved every minute of that day. But to be honest, at the same time, I was happy it was finally over. It had been so emotional, I was completely drained.

I was on such a high the whole time I was in Panama, but that feeling didn't last long once I'd left.

When we returned to the United States, we continued our U.S. tour, and one night, I received a call from my wife. Now of course, I talked to Toi all the time, but this call was different and would change my life.

She was upset when she told me that she'd found phone records of me calling and receiving calls from women.

"I don't know what you're talking about," I lied at first.

But no matter how many times I said that, Toi knew I was lying.

She kept saying over and over, "I don't believe you, Kevin."

And after a while, I decided to come clean. That was a hard decision because I knew once I told her the truth, it would be the end of our marriage, especially because of what we'd went through before.

But I had to tell her. And I did.

"I want a divorce," she said, right away.

She wasn't kidding. This time, she didn't let me talk her into counseling. This time, she didn't listen to anything I had to say. We separated and within three months we were divorced.

That is not something that I wanted because I did love my wife. But I was wrong, and even though Toi forgave me in the end, the consequences were that I lost her as my wife.

Today, Toi and I have a wonderful relationship. We raise Kaydee together as mature adults. We communicate daily and have very few disagreements and no arguments whatsoever. We spend time together, for Kaydee's sake, going out as a family.

Considering that we're divorced, this is the best possible situation. I will always respect Toi and don't blame her for the decision she had to make. The truth of the matter is, I wasn't ready to be married. I had so many unresolved issues and Toi did her best to be understanding.

But, she couldn't handle the way I behaved. She couldn't handle all the women I had, and to be honest she shouldn't have to. Losing her was something I didn't want, but it was what I deserved.

XVIII.

He Never Stopped Smiling

"Challenges are what make life interesting and overcoming them is what makes life meaningful." - Joshua J. Marine

When I was a little kid growing up in Panama, I never knew how far basketball would take me. All I knew was that I was going to do everything I could so that I could get as far as possible with the sport I loved. Throughout my life, it wasn't easy to maintain my focus. But, my goal meant more to me than anything, and my determination was much greater than anything in the world.

Well, basketball took me further than I imagined: To ninety-five countries with an international fan base which includes countless celebrities who I'd admired from afar, but who are now fans of mine, to being a Guinness Book of World Record holder, to playing one-on-one with the best player of all time, Michael Jordan.

Of course, all of that pleases me since I always aspired to make money from basketball. But what has made my job so special is that while I always aspired to have this career, I never realized how I'd be able to use basketball to inspire others.

To me, every time I stepped on the court I was just doing what I loved to do. If I didn't play basketball for a living, I would still play during my free time.

But it wasn't until I began receiving fan mail that I realized my job was more than bouncing a ball on a court. My job healed hearts, brought families together, and it actually inspired individuals to become the best that they could be.

One of the most memorable pieces of fan mail that I ever received came from a lady in the United States. She wrote:

"You made me so happy tonight. You signed my jeans and treated me like no one has before. That was very important to me. I am fighting cancer for the third time. If this is the last thing I do, I will be satisfied. Thank you from the bottom of my heart."

When I read this email, tears poured from my eyes. I was so touched by her taking the time to write me and telling me this. I never knew I could or would have this type of impact on someone's life.

All of us, no matter who we are, no matter what we do for a living, are inspiring someone, somewhere, and we don't even know it. It's so important for us to remember that. That's an even greater reason for us to all take pride in our jobs.

You could be a garbage man, feeling that your job is worthless. Complaining everyday because you have to get up, go out, and pick up trash. But at the same time, there is someone watching you. It may be a homeless man with no job to go to. That homeless man has no money and he's struggling just to find food to eat.

Can you imagine if this homeless man sees you every-day when you get out of your car to start your shift at work? You may think you're just dumping trash, but what you're doing is so much more important to him. He's watching you work! Then, suppose he sees you during your lunch break eating a sandwich? That homeless man wishes he had your job, he wishes he had your life.

That's a lesson that I've learned through my career. We must be grateful for what we have and proud of what we do. If you're unhappy with your job situation, do something about it. Apply for a different position, find another job, but in the meantime continue to do your best where you're at because you never know who may be watching and whom you may be inspiring.

That lesson really hit home for me in 2012 when the Harlem Globetrotters and the National Campaign to Stop Violence asked me to fly to Washington, DC to assist in a national anti-bullying program they were developing. I was part of the creative process, and I was also going to be presenting the program to thousands of students in hundreds of schools all across the United States.

After just a few presentations, I began to realize how big of a problem bullying is in this country. The stories I heard from students, teachers, and parents became real eye-openers for me. I wanted to help fix the problem; I was willing to take on that responsibility. But I didn't know what to do.

After days and weeks of thinking about it, the answer came to me. And it was quite simple.

I got the big idea when I met a twelve-year-old kid named Erick after a game in Tennessee. While I was signing autographs, his mother passed by and whispered in my ear, "He tried to commit suicide." Then she pointed at a young kid.

Her words were so shocking to me, and I looked at the boy she pointed to. Immediately, I was touched because I had my own history with suicide.

I wanted to connect with that boy right away, but I was in the middle of signing autographs. I wanted private time with the boy and his mother, so I told her to go to the Globetrotters website and email me.

"I really want to talk to both of you," I said.

She agreed and that night, I received her email. She explained that Erick had tried to commit suicide numerous times because of the bullying at school. She was so angry because she felt that the school wasn't doing enough to protect her son. Erick was so affected by the bullying that he was taking medication to help him deal with the situation, and he had even stopped attending school.

I responded back to the mom, asked for their phone number, and got her permission to call. A few days later, I spoke with Erick.

He couldn't believe he was really speaking to me on the phone. Can you imagine your favorite sports hero calling you? That's how Erick told me it was for him.

"How are you doing?" I asked him.

"I'm fine, I guess." I heard the sadness in his soft voice.

"Do you want to tell me what's going on?"

He opened up, telling me everything. He explained the whole situation about how the kids at school didn't like him and had bullied him daily when he'd been going to classes. And he told me how he never wanted to go back.

For the first few minutes, I just listened as he talked. And then, we talked together.

"You have to be brave, Erick. You can't let those guys dictate your feelings. They don't have anything to do with you."

He told me how hard it was not having any friends.

"What are you talking about?" I asked him. "I'm your friend and you can call me any time you want."

And that's exactly what happened. Erick and I became friends. He called me from time to time, and sent texts.

Whenever he reached out to me, I got right back to him. All I wanted to do was encourage him, and be there when he needed a listening ear.

After we'd been talking for a couple of months, I invited Erick and his mom and dad to visit me in Dallas. I was looking forward to the weekend with them, but what was interesting was that every day, up until the day they were to leave for Dallas, Erick's mom asked if I still wanted them to come.

"Of course," I always told her.

I guess she just couldn't believe that I was doing this. I was actually going to spend the weekend with them. For me, this wasn't anything out of the ordinary. I was just using my time and spending it with someone who I felt would benefit from being with me and talking to me. Spending this time with Erick was the right thing to do.

They arrived on that Friday evening and we made plans to meet on Saturday at Six Flags.

"We'll spend the whole day together," I told them.

I took Kaydee with me, who was about seven years old and I'm telling you, we all had a blast. Erick's mom said that she couldn't remember the last time she'd seen Erick smile so much.

I wanted the day to be all about Erick. So, I got on the rides with him. Talked to him, laughed with him. We ate together. We hung out as if we'd known each other for years. As if we were good old buddies.

The next day, I invited him to go to the gym so that we could play our favorite sport - basketball, of course.

We played one-on-one, and of course I had to beat him a few games. But I didn't let him leave without him winning a game. I lost the last game as a gift to him. (Shhhh...don't tell him.) Just to see his joy was wonderful.

My goal was to make him smile, and at least for that weekend, he smiled. I wanted him to not think about the negatives that were part of his life.

It worked. Actually, it worked more than I ever thought it   would.

As Erik and I continued to communicate, Erick was transforming, he was growing. His confidence increased, he went back to school, his grades got much better, his basketball skills improved, and he started to put in a lot of time in one of his other favorite hobbies - making and producing music.

It was so rewarding for me to hear the updates from Erick. It was so rewarding to know that I was making a difference.

Three years after we first met, I got the chance to see Erick and his family once again in Tennessee at another game. I told them to meet me after the game backstage so that we could talk and catch up.

When I saw Erick I just couldn't believe it. Of course, he was bigger and taller, that was to be expected in the three years that had passed. But it was his whole attitude that impressed me. Everything about him was different and I noticed right away. He walked with his head high, he looked in my eyes when he spoke in a voice and tone that was filled with confidence. And, he talked about his life, how great it was, how happy he was.

I just stood there listening, and I'm telling you, I had to fight to hold back the tears. Behind him, his mom beamed; she was so proud of her son. And it was a proud moment for me, too.

This is an example of basketball taking me someplace I never imagined. If I had not been playing basketball, I would have never met Erick and wouldn't have had the chance to impact his life the way I did.

And like I said, it was Erick who led me to the big idea. A big idea, that is really rather small, and quite simple. It's just for me to be there for those who reach out to me if I'm able to. I might not be able to reach all, but if I can reach a few and have results like Erick, that would be phenomenal.

So, that's what I started doing. Erick became just one of the amazing stories. I saw similar changes in other kids whose parents contacted me. And after I reached out to them, just like I'd done with Erick, I was able to encourage these young kids who were being bullied. I was able to inspire them and I know that you can inspire others, too. Never forget that.

Interacting with and talking to kids and their parents has taught me so much about bullying. Those same kids and parents inspired me to create my own bullying prevention program that I call "S.TO.P. the Bullying". It's a lot of fun and very rewarding to travel to schools around the world, giving tools on bullying prevention that actually work.

There were so many other goals and passions that I wanted to pursue, and that's why after ten years with the

Harlem Globetrotters, I retired. I felt that I'd reached the highest level possible with the team and it was time to move on.

I wanted to pursue my passion to motivate people, to help others reach their full potential. So today, I do a lot of corporate motivational speaking via www.kevindaleyspeaks.com. But while I love the adults, my heart is with children and I visit many schools, often being contacted by the administrators through my website www.stopthebullying911.com

That's the one thing that is never going to change - the love I have for children and the passion I have to help them. I've started a foundation, The Kevin Daley Youth Foundation, to help as many children as I can who are in need. My foundation comes to the aid of children who are not only being bullied, but who have other issues: like thoughts of suicide, or being abused. I am so excited about my foundation and the good that is going to come out of this - helping thousands of kids.

Now that I'm no longer playing basketball professionally, I'm able to take the time for another interest of mine - acting. I have a few projects in the making right now and I feel really good about them.

I have to say that I'm really happy with this journey I've taken, very pleased where my life has taken me. Yes, I made some mistakes along the way, but I have always learned from those mistakes. And the misfortunes that I've experienced have only served to mold me into a stronger individual.

My life is filled with blessings, the primary one being my beautiful daughter. She is the major driving force in my life. She is the reason why I must and will succeed in whatever lies in front of me. So I look forward to what is ahead with open eyes and a joyful heart. I know I will enjoy the ride of this next stage of my life. And I'm really looking forward to it. When my life finally comes to an end I want people to say, *"He never stopped smiling!"*

XIX.

21 KEYS TO SUCCESS

"The common idea that success spoils people by making them vain, egotistic and self-complacent is erroneous; on the contrary, it makes them for the most part, humble, tolerant and kind. Failure makes people cruel and bitter."-
W. Somerset Maugham, author

S uccess has a different meaning for everyone. Some people believe that success is measured by how much money you have or what type of car you drive. Although that could be a measurement of financial success, it doesn't tell the entire meaning of the word. Success is found in all areas of life including health, career, spiritual, emotional, as well as financial.

Before you are able to achieve success, you need to define what success means to YOU.

In my story, I achieved success when I accomplished my longtime goal of getting paid for playing basketball. My first check was only $1,000, but at that moment that $1,000 check was worth a million dollars to me. After that achievement, I set more goals for myself and as I accomplished those goals I became more and more successful. You may be successful right now and not even know it. I have put together *21 Keys to Success* that I believe are necessary to be successful in any field, in any part of your life. Pay especially close attention to the first three keys. I call them the 3D's. I truly believe that every successful person had to apply at least these three keys to get where they are today.

21 Keys to Success

1. Dedication

To me, dedication is one of the most important keys to success. Without dedication and passion, you will quit at the first sign of adversity. You will quit when you shouldn't quit. It is very hard to give up on something if you are dedicated to it. My dedication and passion for basketball had me on the court every New Years Eve, right after midnight shooting baskets. I could have been doing lots of other things, but I was dedicated to basketball.

2. Desire

You have to have a desire to do whatever it takes for you to succeed. Every goal you set for yourself starts with you having the desire for whatever it is that you want. It also helps if you develop a love what it is that you want to succeed in.

3. Discipline

As you make your way toward success, you will be challenged with big obstacles as well as small ones. You must have the discipline to stay on track. Without discipline to do all the things necessary to achieve your goal, it is almost impossible to achieve success.

4. Hang around successful people.

Successful people are successful for a reason. Hang around them if you ever get a chance. Don't be afraid to ask questions. Successful people will share how they got to their level. After my college basketball career, I would play with and against NBA players. I would watch and learn from their work habits on the basketball court. And then, I took the lessons I learned and applied them to my own career.

5. Be bold and courageous.

You cannot be afraid of rejection or afraid of failure. You have to be very bold and courageous and knock down walls that are put in front of you. Success will never come easy; you have to fight for it.

6. Give 100% effort

Anything you want to achieve is worth and deserves 100% of your effort. Do not cut yourself short by giving anything less than 100%. If you find that you can't give

100%, don't do it. Don't move forward until you can give it your all.

7. Avoid negative people

Negative people will bring you down and make you believe that your goal is not worth it or is unattainable. Do not listen to them. As the matter of fact, use their negativity as motivation to get where you want to be.

8. Stay motivated

It is very important to stay motivated, and sometimes in the middle of the battle, that can be difficult. To stay motivated, read stories of people who have reached the goal you want to reach. You can also find people who have the same goal and you can work together. Motivate each other. Motivation will keep you going on those days when you feel like giving up.

9. Don't be afraid to fail

You cannot let the fear of failure stop you. To me, you only fail when you don't even attempt to succeed. Being afraid of failure is a normal emotion for every person on the planet. How you get past that fear is the determining factor between failing and succeeding. Getting past that fear is what separates successful people from those who are not successful. Believe in yourself and the desire burning within you.

10. Be patient

Most people don't succeed over night. Be patient with yourself, the people around you and the process it takes to succeed. Know that success is ahead. Believe that it will happen in its proper time.

11. Have a good attitude

When people see your good attitude they are going to want to help you succeed. Staying positive and surrounding yourself with friends that share a positive attitude will help you succeed.

12. Be thankful

You need to be thankful for not only your accomplishments, but also your failures. Having a grateful attitude is important. It will help you stay humble, which in turn will help you continue striving for the ultimate in success. The more thankful you are, the more you will keep getting things to be thankful for.

13. Set daily goals

It is very important to set small daily goals that will work toward the big goal. These smaller goals will help you visualize your accomplishments, and stay encouraged. In addition to helping you progress toward your goal, these smaller goals will keep pushing you closer and closer to your success.

14. Don't settle

Do not settle with almost reaching your goal. Keep going all the way and do not give up till you reach it. If you have a goal of becoming a world-famous chef and you know you have both desire and skill, do not settle with becoming a short order cook at your local family-style restaurant. While that may be a good training ground, do not allow yourself to stay there. Do not lose sight of your ultimate goal.

15. Good habits

We all have bad habits, but to succeed we have to minimize them and create good ones. Doing something positive every day to reach your goal is one good habit you can start that will provide a strong base for success.

16. Take care of yourself

Being successful means taking care of yourself both physically and emotionally. You will need to focus, have energy, and rest. This will help you concentrate and put in the hours required to be successful. Without taking proper care of yourself, you will end up struggling and that will definitely affect achieving your goal.

17. No shortcuts

When you want to succeed, you cannot afford to take short cuts. Taking shortcuts often leads to imperfections and inadequacies. Always strive for the best, even if it requires more time and effort. There are no short cuts on the road to success.

18. Relax

While being determined is important, do not be so hard on yourself that you become critical of every move you make. Allow some room for mistakes, and be flexible. If you start getting too stressed, relax and find an outlet. My outlet today is my daughter. When I start getting overwhelmed with everything that I'm dealing with, thinking of her or playing with her brings me back to a happy state of mind.

19. Study

No matter what your goal for success is, you must set aside time to study. Take time to read, research, and ask many questions. The more you learn the better. Successful people are continuous learners.

20. Law of attraction

I am a big believer in the Law of Attraction. Whatever you think about, you shall receive into your life. If you think good thoughts, you will receive good things. Knowing this law, you should think as if you have reached your goal already. Act as if you've achieved it. Feel the emotions that come with that success. Be happy! As happy as you will be when you do reach your goals.

21. Have fun

This one element is often forgotten in the process of attaining success. Keep the process fun. Do not get so consumed in the things that you must do to succeed that you can't find a way to enjoy the journey. Do not get me wrong, the process of succeeding is very serious, but it doesn't mean that we can't have fun while doing it. Success should always be fun for you and those around you.